SEXUALITY, FAITH
CONVERS.

— Part One —

"Stephen Elmes has produced a fine resource that offers a biblically grounded, sensitive and compassionate approach to a difficult issue. His discussion is faithful to the moral vision of the New Testament and rooted in the practical realities of pastoral ministry… a genuinely original piece of work."

Joshua T. Searle, Tutor in Theology and Public Thought, Spurgeon's College

"Stephen Elmes' careful, caring, and thoughtful approach to this charged topic is not only rooted in a readiness to listen to different views but also to accurately represent them. What emerges is a model of biblically faithful, pastorally involved engagement that points a way forward not only on this issue but on many others."

Mark Greene, Executive Director of the London Institute for Contemporary Christianity (LICC)

"Steve adopts an unexpected and creative style that will enable a wide range of people to engage with a challenging and sensitive issue in a non-threatening way that also does justice to the Biblical and theological issues that surround it. As attitudes in society change beyond the recognition of previous generations, it is vital that local churches are equipped to engage meaningfully—this will be a vital resource for that task."

Phil Jump, Regional Minister, North Western Baptist Association (NWBA)

Sexuality, Faith & the Art of Conversation

— Part One —

STEPHEN ELMES

creative tension publications

creative tension publications
1 Nelson Cottages, Oakdene Road
Bookham
Surrey KT23 3HD
United Kingdom
Tel: +44(0)1372453243

ISBN 978-1-5272-0964-0

All Scripture references are taken from the Holy Bible, Today's New International Version (TNIV), Cambridge University Press, © International Bible Society, Cambridge 2005.

.

ACKNOWLEDGMENTS

To my family who have lost me for many hours while I have been working on this project—my grateful thanks to them.

To the members of the working group at Bookham Baptist Church—you know who you are!—what a great team.

To those who were prepared to tell their stories for inclusion in this work—my sincere thanks.

To Andy Gill for the superb cover design—what a great job!

For Sara, Katrina, Brendan & Stefan

CONTENTS

CHAPTER 1

Encounter

31ˢᵗ May 2012. I receive a phone call from Dru, a member of the church community I lead. I detect at once the anxiety in her voice: 'Steve, can you come? I'm with Jonathan … he's in such a state… he won't say why… he's asking for you.'

I arrive at the house some minutes later. Jonathan is standing in the hallway, pale and close to tears. I move towards him to offer him a hug. I hold him as the tears begin to fall. Nothing is said.

A little later, as we sit with our drinks in the lounge, Jonathan finds his voice: 'Steve, I can't do this any more… can't hide any longer...'

Jonathan struggles to let the words form on his lips:

'Steve… I'm gay.'

I move to sit next to Jonathan and put my arms around him while he starts to sob. I ask him if he has acted upon his desires. (As I hear my own words, I regret them—how inappropriate, how unhelpful!) He replies that he has not, clearly a little bemused by my question.

'Steve, I have tried to change it, but I can't. I have known since I was young, though I have often denied it to myself and never told anyone. You are the first… I feel terrible... I know how much it offends God. But I can't help it. This is the way I am. I have given my life to Christ, to serve him. Steve, you know my devotion. I love him… but I am wrong inside, and I can't change it.'

I console Jonathan as best I can, speaking of God's love for him. I tell him that his sexuality does not make him any less a child of God, and certainly not an offense to God. I speak of his sexuality as a gift—however broken it might seem to him—a good gift of God. I tell him that his desires do not make him sinful, and that what really matters is how he acts upon those desires, the choices that he makes.

Jonathan is familiar with the distinction often made between orientation and behaviour in discussions about sexuality. He has done the reading and engaged in the debates. Yet, in this moment, all this is of no help at all. This is deeply personal. He feels wretched, *wrong inside*, condemned. He is overwhelmed and in despair. I adjust my counsel to simply assert that God loves him. I say something about a challenging journey ahead, but stress that right now he just needs to know that God does not despise or condemn him; that he stands in the Grace of God—a forgiven man, a precious son, loved forever. I say it over and over in different ways. I feel clumsy and artless in my attempts to help.

We end in prayer together and arrange to meet again soon.

A few days later, Jonathan is sitting opposite me in my office—composed yet visibly exhausted. He tells me of sleepless nights and struggling with feelings of self-hatred and despair. I speak again of God's love and acceptance, and his pleasure in Jonathan's love and desire to please him.

Several conversations later, Jonathan shares with me how he is coming to terms with being loved by God despite his sexual desires. He also shares with me his determination to live a celibate life, and his plan to make a pledge to this end—before God and before the people who know him well.

15 June 2013. Around thirty of us are gathered in the Sanctuary of our church. I am leading the service, which has been meticulously planned by Jonathan. The gathering includes family members and close friends of Jonathan, all people who have been important in his journey of faith. We worship together and follow a liturgy in which

Jonathan proclaims his faith, and vows to live a celibate life, committed to Christ and *forsaking all others*. The echoes of the marriage liturgy are unmistakable.

My friendship with Jonathan continues to this day. He remains celibate, though this is not without considerable personal turmoil and anguish at times. Jonathan suffers bouts of sadness and depression; sometimes the desire for a life-partner seems overwhelming, and the self-denial he has pledged unbearable. Yet he continues to live his vows and is helped by the support of close friends and the Christian community to trust in the love and power of God to hold and sustain him. There is joy in the journey as well as pain. There is a deep communion with the God he worships. There is a path of discipleship that brings purpose and adventure, yet comes—as it does for all followers of Christ—at cost. For Jonathan, one cost of the Christ-led, Christ-shaped life is that he cannot act upon his desire for a committed, intimate relationship with another man. He has submitted to this willingly and knows the joy of surrender, and the fellowship of his Lord; yet lives too with some of his deepest longings unfulfilled.

I have been describing some of what it means for one young man to follow Christ—the shape of his discipleship—according to what he has understood and come to embrace of Christ's call on his life. Now let me pose a provocative question. Is this the shape of discipleship for all who live with same-sex desires? Or, in clearer terms, is celibacy the only legitimate path for those who are attracted to persons of the same sex and seek to follow Christ? A number today are questioning the traditional and time honoured position of the church on this, arguing that discipleship for some might allow a loving, loyal, sexually intimate relationship with someone of the same-sex: a union that has the potential to reveal the way of Christ in the same way that a marriage between a man and woman has.

I wonder how you reacted to Jonathan's story? Take a few moments to be aware of that now...

Next, imagine I had put this short account of Jonathan's experience in a blog (with Jonathan's agreement, of course). What kinds of responses might it draw?

Six Imagined Responses

Take a look at the following imagined reactions, each of them addressed to Jonathan. Perhaps you can identify with one or more of them.

'Jonathan, your courage and perseverance on the path you have chosen inspire me. I know that God is pleased with you for your decision and determination to honour him through a life of celibacy, and he will surely honour you in return. Yours is a costly road and I can only imagine the distress and desolation you sometimes feel—yet I believe it is the right one, and that your obedience to the way of Christ is of inestimable worth, a powerful witness and an encouragement to others who live with same-sex desires.'

'Jonathan, I certainly respect your decision to live a life of self-restraint, and not to act upon your desires. Yet, I wonder if you go far enough? I mean, do you need to settle for living with these disordered desires at all? Does not God have the power to heal you? I believe so. It is surely not God's will for you to be attracted to your own sex, and clearly, as you know, the Bible forbids all sexual relations between men and between women. So why would God leave you this way? I recently read a book about sexual healing that explained how homosexuality (in men) arises from a deficit in a man's relationship with his father, so it's really a misguided way of trying to put that right. The author gave lots of examples of men and women who found freedom through counselling and prayer. I am sure you could find the same.'

4

'Jonathan, I feel so much respect for you, and I really don't want to undermine your commitment. However, I wonder if you really are called to the celibate life, and whether this is the only way you can follow Christ? I know this is contentious, but I do not believe the Bible is as clear on this as some people argue. Yes, I know we are talking about centuries of church teaching that have consistently forbidden homosexual partnerships; yet recently, as you will know, a number of scholars and church leaders have revisited the handful of texts that refer directly to homosexual behaviour, and come to the conclusion that they really have little or nothing to say to those who seek a loving, committed partnership with someone of the same sex. I have found that my own study of the Scriptures—not just those few forbidding texts but also the broader witness of the Bible—have left me open to the possibility that God might bless such partnerships.'

'Jonathan, I am a gay man and have been in a relationship with another man now for five years—we were both brought up in Christian families but lost our faith, as it seemed to us both that we could not square our sexuality and lifestyle with the Bible or what we had grown up believing. Yet, recently, we found a church that welcomed us and made room for us, and both of us have come to believe that God is not angry with us for being gay—in fact, we have recently come to believe that it is possible to be gay and to follow Jesus, and that God is pleased with our love and commitment for each other. It has been a hard road, but worth battling through. Today we have such a sense of peace and of God's blessing on our relationship, and the support and understanding of a loving church family.'

'Jonathan, forgive me but for the life of me I cannot understand why God would deny you the happiness of a loving, life-long relationship. What kind of God would do that? It seems to me that some people are naturally attracted to the same sex and so it is simply a matter of equality and justice that they should be allowed to enjoy a deep and intimate relationship like anyone else—including the sex! Does God really get angry about that? Honestly? In my reading of the gospels I see Jesus welcoming all kinds of people whom others were excluding. He included people who were on the edge of society and got the religious people all riled up in the process. Jonathan, I believe that God is love and that he is reflected wherever love is present.'

'Jonathan, I don't believe in God, and none of this makes any sense to me at all. It seems to me that your religious beliefs are a terrible constraint on your happiness. I really feel for you. In fact, I feel quite angry, and not a little perplexed, at the way the church dictates the terms of your life. I don't really know the Bible, I admit, but I know there are some real horror stories in there and sometimes God comes over as some kind of angry, monstrous being, wiping out people who won't fall in line. Don't get me wrong; I know religion isn't the cause of all our problems, as some argue. I actually have some friends who are Christians and they're good guys—people I really respect. One of them told me that his church was discussing the whole same-sex issue, trying to get a better understanding of it all. I gather there are different viewpoints in the church. From where I stand, I wonder what on earth there is to talk about—either you accept that some people are different and let them get on with their lives or stay in the dark ages. I know that is strong, but come on, live and let live!'

Six imagined responses to Jonathan's story—take a few moments to reflect on what is going on for you right now...

Let me push you a bit further. Ask yourself, which of these responses you most closely relate to. Do any of them make you feel annoyed, or riled, or disturbed in some way? Take a moment to name the emotions.

Perhaps you relate to the last response as someone who does not claim to follow Christ and cannot fathom why Christians get in such a fix about same-sex relationships. Or maybe, though not identifying as a Christian, you instinctively feel that there may be something in what the church has traditionally taught for centuries about homosexuality that makes sense or seems right, despite it not being 'politically correct'.

Whatever is going on for you, if there is some resonance with any of the above, I invite you to read on and engage with a vital conversation. I make this invitation to all who seek to follow Christ and would like some help in working out a faithful response to those who live with same-sex desires; I make it to those who do not identify as Christians, yet would like to get some insight into the conversation going on among Christians; and I make it to those who live with same-sex desires, for whom the outcome of the conversation is deeply personal.

So what can you expect in the pages ahead? Let me set out what is in store, as succinctly as I can.

Four Woven Strands

As you read on, you will find four types of material woven together in this work. The first is the relating of a conversation that took place between February 2014 and October 2014 involving a dozen people who were (and are) members and friends of Bookham Baptist Church. The group was set the task of considering *how a local Baptist church might respond to those who live with same-sex desires and seek to follow Christ.* This was the main research vehicle for a dissertation that I submitted for a master's degree in the summer of 2015.

The second is a set of 'focus pieces' that pick up on elements of the conversation just mentioned, in order to pursue things a little further—such as the different ways in which the Bible is interpreted in relation to same-sex relationships, the contributions of science to our understanding of sexuality, the relationship between sexuality and identity, and so on.

The third is a collection of true-life stories, collected by myself in conversations with a number of individuals and couples. These were included as appendices in the original work, but woven into the main body of the work here.

The fourth is brand new material, not present at all in my dissertation: fictional conversations, between myself and an invented character called Alex, taking place over a series of meetings at a local coffee house. Alex—**not** a real person remember—does not profess to be a follower of Christ, though has some familiarity with the biblical text and the Christian faith, and many questions about both. These conversations are contrived to take place in-between the real-life sessions of the working group, and are designed to provide some explanation of the group's activities, approach and outcomes, along with further exploration of the issues raised, in the manner of a free-flowing discussion. The detail of Alex's non-believing status is important, as he is inclined to ask different kinds of questions to those who share my faith in Christ. This literary device could be perceived in at least two ways. Firstly, as a way of opening up the conversation to those who do not identify as followers of Christ, and secondly, as a way of subjecting the task, approach and outcomes of the working group to some tougher probing and challenging than might occur from within the community of believers. You will see what I mean.

One last thing: throughout this work I have provided some opportunities to pause and reflect along the way, headed *Join the Conversation*. These contain some prompts that might be used by individual readers and/or by a small group meeting to discuss this material. These are intended as a resource and are not compulsory to complete! Use them (or not) as you find helpful.

Well, it's time to get going. Let's begin at the Wild Goose. Let me introduce you to Alex.

CHAPTER 2

Coming to an Arrangement

Wild Goose Coffee House: 1 February 2014—the time is 11:15

Steve is at the counter of the Wild Goose Coffee House, ordering drinks. Alex is sat at one of the tables, answering a text message on his mobile. The café, which can seat around twenty five people, is about half full, so there is a light buzz of conversation mixing with the mellow sound of jazz coming from a very impressive sound system, the pride and joy of the proprietor, who is known as Cass.

CASS: Chocolate on the Cappuccino?

STEVE: Please.

CASS: And milk with the Americano… hot or cold?

STEVE: Hot, and could we have two glasses of water with those?

CASS: Of course, any cakes? All home made, baked today.

STEVE: Not just now, Cass.

CASS: I'll bring your drinks over—you sit yourself down.

Steve joins Alex, patting his shoulder as he sits down opposite him.

STEVE: Hey! Thanks for making the time.

ALEX: Pleasure. Come here often?

STEVE: Possibly too often—I like the atmosphere.

ALEX: Interesting décor.

STEVE: Yes, quite arty, the unfinished look!

(The walls are exposed rough brick, framed and criss-crossed with weathered oak beams.)

ALEX: If I'm honest, part of me wants to get my trowel and go to work on the place!

STEVE: I like it.

Steve and Alex continue chatting about the décor, until...

ALEX: So then, tell me more about this intriguing, or should I say, mysterious proposition of yours.

STEVE: Right, yes, I guess I was a bit cryptic when I called you.

ALEX: Just a bit.

STEVE: Do you remember me telling you about the working group I have set up at church, to explore the issue of same-sex relationships?

ALEX: Sure, I remember—I think I gave you a bit of a hard time about it.

STEVE: As I recall, you said something along the lines that the church was living in the past and hopelessly out of touch with the lives of real people, and that it needed to get over its homophobia and let people get on with their lives.

ALEX: Did I say that?

STEVE: Oh yes! It's engraved in my memory! You also asked me some very penetrating questions and pushed me hard on my responses. Once you'd had your rant, you proved to be very perceptive.

Cass comes to the table and sets down two coffees and two glasses of water.

STEVE: Thanks Cass.

CASS: You're welcome—enjoy. The offer of home-baked cakes is still open.

STEVE: Thanks, we might well take you up on that.

Cass leaves, smiling.

ALEX: So you've come back for more of my vast wisdom?

STEVE: In a way, yes. I would like you to consider being my conversation partner while I lead the working group over the next five or six months. I need someone with whom I can reflect on what is happening to the group and my own journey with all this. I thought you would be great.

ALEX: But, I don't believe in God, well, agnostic at best. I'm certainly not one of your Jesus followers.

STEVE: Not yet.

ALEX: Oh, I see! This is about you trying to convert me!

STEVE: No, not really, I… (*stumbling on his words*)

ALEX: (*Enjoying the moment*) Sure about that?

STEVE: Well, of course I would love you to come to faith in Christ. That's because I think it's the best thing that could happen to anyone…

ALEX: (*Cutting in*) So, all this is basically a ploy: an elaborate way of getting me into your holy club!

STEVE: Honestly Alex, that's not my motivation here. I need a good conversation partner who is not part of the community in which this work is being done. I need someone who will listen well, but will challenge me too, who won't let me get away with any hidden agendas or sleights of hand. I think you have just demonstrated your credentials there!

ALEX: Okay, I think you recovered that—just be warned that I won't be an easy fish to reel in!

STEVE: I can be very patient, my friend… I play the long game. (*Steve gives a mock ominous look.*) Seriously, Alex, it's a good conversation I am after—if you get converted, well that's in God's hands! I did pray about this—I am convinced you're the right person for the job.

ALEX: Okay, so how would it work?

STEVE: We meet here, say twice a month? I tell you a bit about how the group is getting on and what's going on in my head, and you just respond the way you do naturally. We can just see what happens.

ALEX: Okay, so when does your group start?

STEVE: In a couple of weeks—we've got a whole morning together.

ALEX: Will that be a kind of scene-setter?

STEVE: Yes, I want to take the group through some of the materials I have used before with a number of church leadership teams across the region. I'll look to give an overview of the scientific stuff, visit the biblical passages that make reference to same-sex behaviour—including different interpretations of these—and then get into some case studies, to really get them working. I'll also make sure we have time to discuss how we use our time in subsequent sessions—to fashion our methodology.

ALEX: So, who is in your group? I mean, how did you choose the participants?

STEVE: I sent out a paper to the members of the church, and a few others who regularly attend.

ALEX: So not everyone who comes is a member?

STEVE: That's correct—maybe I can come back to that?

ALEX: Ok, but don't forget. I smell the odious scent of exclusivity!

STEVE: I'll come back to it, I promise. As I was saying, I sent out a paper to members and others, inviting them to apply to be involved in a theological and pastoral reflection that would run over about six months. I asked those who wanted to apply to look at five summary viewpoints on same-sex relationships, and to indicate which of them was closest to their own. My intention was to bring together a group that reflected the whole range of viewpoints: from a very conservative position that would see in all cases the need for repentance and healing, through to what some would describe as a liberal position that argues for the full acceptance and blessing of same-sex relationships, putting them on a par with a marriage between a man and a woman.

ALEX: Wow, you have both those views present in your church?

STEVE: Absolutely, and all the positions in between. You might like to look at the five views before we next meet. I'll send them to you, along with the paper I sent out.

ALEX: So you're going to have a potentially explosive mix.

STEVE: I guess, although I have not been able to recruit anyone from viewpoint A: the most conservative view.

ALEX: Disappointing. Won't that limit your conversation and the validity of its outcome?

STEVE: It is disappointing, but not surprising. Those who hold this view tend to be bemused by the conversation in that they see nothing to discuss. They would hold that the Bible is clear about this subject—that homosexuality is unambiguously denounced: from the horrific tale of Sodom and Gomorrah through to the words of St. Paul in the New Testament, homosexual acts are roundly condemned. Not that the word, 'homosexual' actually appears in the Bible, but it is clear that same-sex erotic behaviour is in view in the handful of texts in question.

ALEX: So, if the Bible is so clear and categorical, what *is* there to talk about? Are the other views just various attempts to wriggle out of the plain sense of those texts? Maybe you just have to accept what's there and then decide if you're going to let those ancients tell us all how to live? Frankly, perhaps you just need to face the fact that the Bible has a few clangers in it. Do you defend it at all points, or come to terms with some parts being, how shall I say, less enlightened? I mean, haven't women been kept in place for centuries by the chauvinism of the Biblical writers—especially St. Paul?

STEVE: You know more than you've let on, I think. However, you might be surprised if you were to take a closer look at St. Paul's writings—he is not the chauvinist many take him for. In fact, the keeping down of women has had more to do with how Paul's words have been interpreted than with what he intended. Understood in the context he was writing in, Paul's words are actually quite liberating.

ALEX: So it's all in the interpretation? Not wriggling out of the obvious meaning?

STEVE: Yes, interpretation—though I've seen some wriggling in my time, and probably done some! The point is, this set of ancient writings that we receive and honour as God's Word, is not some kind of instruction manual for living—even though it is sometimes portrayed like that. It contains history, law-books, stories aplenty, letters, songs, and so on. All these diverse writings were produced in a very different world, or I should say worlds, to our own. So we cannot always assume that what we understand is exactly what was intended. We need to take care—to 'mind the gap'.

ALEX: So even the clangers might ring true if you spend some time on them?

STEVE: I like that—yes.

ALEX: Even so, your conversation is going to be limited by the absence of those who hold the most conservative views.

STEVE: Yes, I accept that. My hope is that we can gather them into the conversation later.

ALEX: Seems more likely that they will be alienated by an outcome that did not involve them in the proce—if you get what I mean.

STEVE: You might be right.

ALEX: Fancy another coffee?

STEVE: Yes, and perhaps some cake?

ALEX: I'm on to it.

EMAIL FROM STEVE TO ALEX

Sent 23:00 the same day

Hi Alex,

Really enjoyed talking with you yesterday evening, and delighted that you are willing to be my conversation partner over the next six months or so. The Wild Goose is a great setting and serves some very good coffee—all very conducive! As promised, I am sending you the paper I sent out to our church members and regulars, along with the 'five viewpoints' that accompanied it and helped me to select the group. Happy reading! I look forward to hearing what you think when we next meet.

Steve

Attachment 1—Letter to Members

CAN YOU HELP ME WITH MY RESEARCH PROJECT (MTh)?

Many of you will be aware that I am studying for a Masters Degree in Applied Theology. Next year (2014) I will be carrying out some research that will be written up as my dissertation. The title I am working to is

How might a local Baptist Church respond to those of homosexual orientation seeking to live as followers of Christ?

Over the last four years or so, I have led a number of one-day seminars to help leaders and congregations within our denomination grapple with this issue. For these I have used the excellent resources prepared by the Baptist Union Working Group on Human Sexuality. It has been a rewarding experience for me to facilitate some very searching conversations and to see Christians with different views and experiences engaging so well with what is, without doubt, one of the most contentious and emotive issues of our day. Many of you will recall that I led one of these days in Bookham a few years ago. The day went very well, yet left a strong sense that more would be needed to work through the outcomes of the time we spent together. It was clear that there were a range of viewpoints and convictions among us (as is the case every time I lead this seminar), and the question left begging was how these differences might translate into pastoral practice.

This challenge is the burden of my research. What I plan to do is assemble a working group of between 8—12 people, drawn from our church community and representing a range of viewpoints. This group will be invited over six months to take part in a theological and pastoral conversation that will be pursued between February and July of next year (2014), meeting on five or six occasions. Two of these will be whole days, and the others around 2-3 hours each. Our objective will be to craft a pastoral response, arising from our discussions, to be submitted to the church meeting in July 2014.

If you would like to be involved in this group, I would love to hear from you. I have devised a simple application form (see below) for those who are interested. This makes reference to a summary of five Christian viewpoints, which you are asked to read and to indicate which of them is closest to your own view at this time. This is to help me to ensure that the 8—12 people invited to be on the working group represent a range of views and convictions relating to the issue, as well as a good balance of age and gender. Application does not guarantee involvement for this reason. Be assured that I will not pass on your views to anyone else. Which leads me to add that there will be strict confidentiality concerning what group members share in sessions—including the final report to the church meeting (individual views will not be disclosed).

In addition to the discussions of the working group, I will be seeking to set up and carry out some one to one interviews with church leaders who have taken part with their leaders or congregations in the seminars I mentioned above, and also with a number of individuals outside of our church community who identify as both gay and Christian. Some outcomes of these interviews, with due regard for confidentiality, will be fed into the working group discussions to inform and enrich our work together.

Stephen Elmes

Please fill in your details in the grid below and respond to the questions that follow as appropriate.

Name	
Gender	
Age	
Address	
Telephone No.	
Mobile No.	
Email Address	

I have read the summary views on same-sex partnerships (separate document) and my view at present is closest to (please enter A, B, C, D or E).

I would like to add that (please add any further comments below, continuing overleaf if needed):

I would be prepared to give two Saturdays (9 am to 4 pm) and four evening sessions to meet between 1st February and 31st July 2014 (please tick the box if so).

Signed.................................... Date........................

Please note that this form will only be viewed by Stephen Elmes and his research supervisor for the purpose of seeking a balance of ages, genders and views within the working group. It will then be kept in a secure place.

Please print, complete and return this form to Stephen Elmes.

ATTACHMENT 2

FIVE CHRISTIAN VIEWS ON SAME-SEX RELATIONSHIPS

A

Scripture condemns homosexual practice and the church should always regard it as sinful. Furthermore, sexual attraction to someone of the same sex should be repented of and healing sought from such desires. It is contradictory to speak of being a 'gay Christian', since the path to holiness must involve the transformation of disordered sexuality within a loving Christian community.

B

Scripture clearly denounces homosexual acts, but says nothing about sexual orientation. A distinction must be made between orientation and practice, otherwise those who experience same-sex desires will conclude that their temptations make them unacceptable to God, which is against the grain of biblical truth. A celibate homosexual is no more sinful than a celibate heterosexual, both of whom must learn restraint and seek to live a life of purity. However, it may be that, within the loving and prayerful support of a Christian community, someone with a homosexual orientation can experience healing (a change of orientation), opening up the possibility of (heterosexual) marriage.

C

Scripture's condemnation of homosexual practice seems to have in view unloving acts that exploit others and/or involve the perversion of sexual desire. These include gang rape, pederasty[1], temple prostitution and the search by heterosexuals for illicit sexual thrills. It is difficult, therefore, to make a decision about the acceptability of a loving, exclusive, same-sex partnership from the few biblical texts that make reference to homosexuality directly. However, the biblical norm from Creation onwards is marriage between a man and a woman, and no alternative is envisaged apart from celibacy, which is given high status in the writings of Paul in the New Testament. Celibacy, for both homosexuals and heterosexuals, therefore, needs to be recovered as a high calling, and re-valued by the church community over and against a culture that sees sexual fulfilment as a right and a necessity. At the same time, great care should be taken to avoid putting pressure on those who are homosexual to seek and experience change in their sexual orientation, as this typically brings more feelings of guilt than healing. As for the idea that a good heterosexual marriage will bring about the needed change, there are many casualties that say otherwise.

D

While the Bible's references to homosexual practice most likely refer to behaviour that is unloving and exploitative, the Creation narratives make it clear that God's original purpose held no alternative beyond heterosexual marriage, except celibacy (by implication and developed in later parts of Scripture). However, the fall of mankind brought disorder to creation, and homosexuality is only one example of this. Since we believe in a God who acts constantly to redeem his fallen creation, we might legitimately ask how he might work with those whose sexual orientation is homosexual and seemingly unlikely to change. We experience God working to transform our broken-ness in many creative ways. Could a loving, committed, homosexual partnership be one of those ways, even if not within the original purpose of creation?

E

The condemnations in Scripture of homosexual practice are aimed at unloving, exploitative acts, and no prohibition is found concerning loving, committed homosexual relationships. What Scripture everywhere affirms is covenant loyalty, and this is given its clearest affirmation in marriage (between a man and a woman). However, it can also be expressed in faithful, loving and monogamous homosexual partnerships between people of pronounced same-sex orientation, and such are worthy of the blessing of the church as an expression of God's purpose for human community, which is loving and committed human relationship.

JOIN THE CONVERSATION...

This is the first of nine opportunities to pause and reflect. The prompts below can be used to aid individual reflection and/or to facilitate a group discussion. The first prompt is the same for each time, and may be all that is needed to get you thinking or talking. If you prefer to simply read on, please feel free to do so.

1 What are your thoughts and feelings about what you have read? It may help you to write them down. If you are in a group context, take time to let each person share, listening carefully to one another.

2 How did you react to Jonathan's story at the start of chapter 1? Which of the six imagined responses did you most closely relate to? Did any of them disturb or provoke you in any way?

3 What do you make of Alex?

4 What do you think of the idea of setting up a group within a church to discuss the issue of same-sex relationships? Could you see this working in your own context? Could you imagine such a group tackling other issues in the life of a church or in another organisation?

5 Take another look at the summary views (A–E) on pages 21–23. Can you locate where you stand at present among these views? It may be that you are in between two of them, or torn between two or more.

For those of you who are eager to know more about how the working group went about their task, the next chapter is for you.

CHAPTER 3

So You Call This Research?

Wild Goose Coffee House: 8 February 2014—the time is 14:34

Steve and Alex have their coffees and have been chatting for about half an hour as we join them.

ALEX: So, down to business. You wanted to talk about your methodology.

STEVE: Yes, I think I need to talk it through.

ALEX: Go for it.

STEVE: Well, in essence, as you know, the approach is to hold a conversation, spread over five or six months, and to see what happens. In a way that's it.

ALEX: It doesn't sound very rigorous.

STEVE: Rigorous?

ALEX: I mean disciplined, perhaps. I associate research with carefully chosen questions and controlled conditions. You know, making sure that everyone is asked the same thing in the same way, no leading questions, watching out for the bias of the interviewer. Just having a conversation seems, if you'll forgive me saying, a bit free and easy. How on earth will you measure the outcomes? And how can you trust them?

STEVE: You're talking about the 'scientific method'—the classic approach of western rationalism.

ALEX: Am I?

STEVE: Yes, it comes from a deep commitment to reason as our way of knowing what can be known about the universe.

ALEX: Sounds good to me!

STEVE: 'I think, therefore I am.'

ALEX: Yes, I've heard that one. I guess that your faith in God falls outside of that approach?

STEVE: Well, yes and no. Certainly the fathers of rationalism made reason the arbiter of truth—accepting as valid knowledge only what could be proved by reason and by careful investigation. The authority of the Bible was thereby brought into question. Yet many Christian thinkers have sought to establish that belief in God is reasonable, and to set out proofs of his existence by rational means.

ALEX: Like the watch!

STEVE: The watch?

ALEX: I remember my old religious studies teacher talking about how we look at a watch with all its intricate mechanisms and assume that there must be a watchmaker, and that the universe is like that.

Design points to a designer.

STEVE: Yes, that kind of thing. There's a lot more where that came from.

ALEX: And the scientific method?

STEVE: It's the application of rationality by means of careful investigation. So, a theory might be formulated about how things work…

ALEX: *(interrupting)* What things?

STEVE: All kinds of things. It could be how a gas reacts under heat or pressure, how rats behave in a laboratory, or how people respond to a drug or a situation or a set of questions. The idea is to create the conditions to measure the response (of gas, rats or people), in order to prove or disprove the theory. This usually means attempting to isolate what you are trying to measure, so that other factors don't get in the way, or at least reducing the variables at play to just a few. It's also important to ensure that the experiment is repeated in exactly the same way with some kind of control group in place (such as five people taking a drug being tested, and five taking a placebo). Add to this the vital 'critical distance' of the researcher—making sure that the researcher's own biases and assumptions do not influence the outcomes—and you have the scientific method.

ALEX: Now, that's what I call rigorous and disciplined. Makes your conversation sound a bit shoddy as far as research goes.

STEVE: Yet, a conversation is what is needed, giving people the freedom to explore, react to each other's ideas, and work things out together. A set of carefully constructed questions with multiple-choice answers would lose the dynamic I am looking for.

ALEX: I can see that, but can you really call what you are doing research? Just letting people talk?

STEVE: I believe so. The scientific method is not the only approach to understanding the world. In fact, it has come under a fair amount of criticism in recent decades—especially in its application to the social sciences.

ALEX: You mean that people are not so easy to work out as gases and lab rats?

STEVE: Yes, but also that the scientific method misses, or is ill equipped to get at, something fundamental about human beings.

ALEX: Which is?

STEVE: That we are social by nature.

ALEX: Aren't rats social too?

STEVE: Yes, but there is a crucial difference. In our attempts to understand the world and find meaning, we are disposed to interact with one another. Some would say that meaning is socially constructed, within the context of the history and cultures that shape us. We experience life with others, and those others have a profound affect on how we understand and talk about things.

ALEX: And the scientific method can't measure this?

STEVE: Well, with its whole approach of isolating what is being studied, say through carefully worded, closed questions to individuals in carefully controlled conditions, the approach simply misses out on the potential of human interaction to discover and learn together. Whereas, if you get a dozen people together and get them talking…

ALEX: Okay, but it still sounds a long way from a credible research approach to me. Surely the further you move away from those carefully worded questions the more unmanageable the outcomes. How on earth do you analyse a free-flowing conversation?

STEVE: Perhaps it is not so much about management and analysis as about paying attention to what emerges?

ALEX: You'll have to unpack that one.

STEVE: Okay, let's back up a little first. There are many approaches to research that have moved very definitely away from treating people like gases and rats. Carefully controlled interviews are abandoned in favour of facilitated conversations in which people are less self-conscious and so more able to be caught up in working things out together. Outcomes are often wide open. There is no theory, necessarily, to prove or disprove. It is a case of 'let's just see where this goes.' Such approaches spell a kind of liberation from the strict controls and narrow channels of the scientific method, which, when applied to human beings are not always fit for purpose.[1]

ALEX: I get the point, but still wonder if such human interactions, rich as they may be, can produce anything dependable or worth writing up in a journal?

STEVE: Okay, let's think about our conversation here and now. We are flowing freely, without the aid of a multiple-choice questionnaire, yes?

ALEX: Or a safety net!

STEVE: So, what is happening as we talk?

ALEX: I'm checking out your research methodology—posing

questions, looking for the holes in your case.

STEVE: Exactly. Which means that you can influence me, so that my thinking might be adjusted or even radically changed.

ALEX: And mine too?

STEVE: Of course. When two or more people engage in conversation the potential for such change is there. To put it more technically, a 'fusion of horizons'[2] occurs which holds the possibility, or likelihood, of adjustments—small or large—to each of our world views.

ALEX: Sounds a very grand way to describe a chat over a cappuccino!

STEVE: You are right—quite pretentious!

ALEX: So, can I guess where you might go next?

STEVE: Be my guest!

ALEX: You'll be arguing, I think, that the researcher who conducts this kind of research…

STEVE: *(interrupting)* Call it 'social constructivist' if you like.

ALEX: If I must… the social constructivist approach will, I think, be interested not so much in the views that each participant brings to the conversation, but in what happens when those views are shared and brought into interaction.

STEVE: Spot on, yes! So a researcher might look for points of agreement as well as points of disagreement; for learning and development in individuals and the group as a whole; and for insights and ways forward that are fashioned from the interaction of the group.

ALEX: So this is really about problem solving.

STEVE: That sounds a bit narrow: it is about reaching understanding together and discovering how best to go forward.

ALEX: Sounds like problem solving.

STEVE: I prefer discernment.

ALEX: Call it what you will, but I think I am sensing a problem—a sizeable pitfall.

STEVE: Tell me.

ALEX: Well, it's to do with power and influence. Think about our conversation, and tell me where the power lies.

STEVE: What do you mean?

ALEX: Which of us is in the most powerful position to influence the other? Who is it that initiated this conversation? Whose agenda is driving it? Who is the most knowledgeable about the whole business of research? Who has done the reading and the thinking ahead of time?

STEVE: Yes, I see.

ALEX: Now transfer this thought to your research group. Who has the power there? Who initiated and set the agenda? Who is leading the group?

STEVE: So you're saying…

ALEX: *(interrupting)* I am saying that you are in a position of great influence, and I don't see any checks and balances. What is to stop you, by dint of your greater knowledge and your powers of persuasion, from bringing the group round to your viewpoint?

STEVE: I take your point. Let's think about this. One way to counter the dangers of undue influence would be to retreat to the 'critical distance' of the scientific method—to lead the project in such a way that my own ideas, thoughts and feelings are kept well out of the interactions of the group.

ALEX: So you sit in the corner and watch from afar?

STEVE: Or maybe behind one-way glass, just like in the police dramas!

ALEX: Perhaps a bit drastic!

STEVE: Yes, but imagine that is how I proceed. Do you really think this would take my influence away from the group? Would it protect them completely from how I think and feel about the issue in hand? Remember, I would still be setting up the activities of the group and processing the outcomes of their conversations. Plus, they would undoubtedly be affected as a group by the ominous feeling of being watched.

ALEX: Like lab rats!

STEVE: Precisely.

ALEX: So how do you eliminate your biases, whether behind glass or not?

STEVE: You're assuming it's a good thing to do that.

ALEX: Well, isn't it?

STEVE: Maybe when studying gases, but not so much when trying to understand anything to do with human beings. More to the point, the notion of eliminating all researcher bias is highly questionable. Can any of us really come at anything with complete objectivity? And even if we could, is it really the ideal many assume it is? Let me to try to turn this around, and suggest that what I bring to the conversation—including my leadership, ideas, feelings, experiences, and so on—might actually be valuable to the group and the process we are committed to.

ALEX: Okay, that's fair, but what about undue influence?

STEVE: I think that the best check on that will be a combination of self-awareness—on my part—and upfront honesty in my dealings with the group.

ALEX: That sounds noble, but I think I would look for a few more checks and balances.

STEVE: Okay, let me add a few others. Firstly, there is the task we are committed to, which has been clearly stated. We are together for a purpose: to discuss how a local church might respond (well) to those who live with same-sex desires and seek to follow Christ. We are accountable as a group to attend to this task, and if I take us too far from this goal, the group is bound to let me know. What is more, the task, as defined, has been presented to members of the church, who in turn have commissioned us to undertake it and to report back to them. Secondly, the group has been set up quite deliberately to bring together a good range of viewpoints. Thirdly, there will be regular reporting. I intend to track or capture the main contours of the conversation each time we meet, and send my notes to the members of the group for verification. In addition, I will be inviting group members to record their own reflections on the sessions.

ALEX: I begin to feel reassured.

STEVE: There's more—much more. I haven't mentioned the Baptist way of being church yet.

ALEX: The Baptist way?

STEVE: We are a local Baptist church, and that commits us to a particular way of practicing our faith in Christ—especially when it comes to making decisions together.

ALEX: Go on, I must confess I know next to nothing about what makes your kind of church any different from all the others. Frankly it's all a bit bewildering from the outside.

STEVE: Perhaps I could give you a bit of an idea here and now. How about I tell you a story?

ALEX: Why not.

Alex sits back in his chair. Steve adopts the pose of a story teller, bringing as much drama and pathos to the moment as he can muster…

MUSINGS FROM A PRISON CELL

1614. Newgate Prison. John Smyth summoned his soul once more to pray, quoting the psalms from memory: 'Why my soul, are you downcast? Why so disturbed within me? Put your hope in God, for I will yet praise him, my Saviour and my God (Psalm 43:5).'

John cast his gaze around his cell and drew his blanket tight around him. His chest wheezed as he drew in breath, and he shivered against the cold. As often happened in the darkness of night, he drifted into memories, remembering his life before captivity. He recalled the years in Amsterdam, with his good friend Thomas Helwys. They had moved there from London with a small band of believers in 1608, to escape the disapproval of the church—the Church of England—with its intolerance of those who gathered to worship outside its dominion. Those who worshipped outside the C of E were known as separatists, and life was not easy for them. Amsterdam had offered freedom: to think and to explore what it might mean to rediscover an authentic church community, following Christ together. For it had become clear to John and Thomas that the established church had lost its moorings. The King's headship of the church threatened to displace its true Lord, Jesus Christ. The priesthood wielded power over the people. And many who attended services were far from being true disciples of Jesus. Nominal Christianity was rife.

John recalled the night they baptised each other, Thomas and he, in Amsterdam. It had seemed such a daring yet freeing act. In this they had no doubt been influenced by their conversations with the Mennonites, who practiced baptism only for those who had made a clear profession of faith in Jesus Christ. This, of course, put them more at odds with the established church, with its practice of infant baptism. The church regarded these 're-baptisers' as heretics. John and Thomas went on to baptise all the believers with them in Amsterdam.

In 1612 came the return to England, to establish the very first English Baptist Church in Spitalfields, London. John recalled and felt again the heady excitement of it: here was their opportunity to really live out their vision of the church—a local gathering of baptised believers, a holy priesthood together, ministers all, seeking to work out in freedom what pleased their Lord. It was a radical and exciting vision. It wasn't long before John found himself in prison.

John sat up and swung himself around to face the barred window that let the early morning light so sparingly into his dank cell. He lifted his head and uttered more words from the psalms: 'Send me your light and your faithful care, let them lead me; let them bring me to your holy mountain, to the place where you dwell (Psalm 43: 3).' He looked down at his right hand and remembered the feel of the quill and the sensation of his hand brushing against rough paper as he scratched out his thesis: 'A short declaration of the mystery of iniquity'. It was a call for freedom of conscience and he had dedicated it to King James. For this he languished now in Newgate Prison.

John died in prison, four years after his sentence. However, the church carried on and the movement of Baptists in Great Britain grew. Some years later an Act of Tolerance was passed (1869) which guaranteed freedom of religious worship for all.

STEVE: What do you think?

ALEX: Fascinating—I didn't know any of that. A little history lesson never goes amiss—though I think you told it with some artistic licence.

STEVE: Of course, no one really knows what went on in John Smyth's head in Newgate Prison, but I thought it might help to imagine his thoughts and memories, as a way of bringing those events to life.[3]

ALEX: So how is your relationship with your local Anglican vicar? I mean, in view of the history. Are you sworn enemies?

STEVE: *(Laughing)* By no means! We are the best of friends! As I think you know.

ALEX: Sure, it's never good to bear a grudge!

STEVE: The truth is, the Anglican church has long moved on from persecuting Baptists!—the kind of reaction, incidentally, that all Christian traditions are capable of in the face of a new movement. I have a theory that, in the long run, such movements have a way of forcing more established expressions of the church to re-evaluate things. The road can be bumpy, even perilous, for a time, yet ultimately reform or renewal in one part of the church brings a wider good for the whole of Christ's church.

ALEX: So is that what is happening over same-sex relationships?

STEVE: Well, it is certainly true that all the Christian traditions (or denominations) are having to grapple with the issue, responding, in part, to those among their numbers who are championing more affirming stances. What I would highlight is that Baptists have a distinctive way of doing this that reflects our heritage—which is why I told you the story of the early Baptists.

ALEX: You'll need to explain that. I still haven't really made the connection between your chatty research group and what you call your heritage.

STEVE: Okay. Do you remember how the early Baptists refuted the authority of King James over the church, and of the priests too, who, it seemed to them were lording it over the people? This was not just a rebellious stand against authority, but rather an assertion of the sole

Lordship (authority) of Jesus Christ, who alone was (and is) Lord of his church. The early Baptists lived in community under the direct governance of their Lord, seeing no need for a priest as such. In fact, they regarded all members of the church as priests, with equal access to God through Jesus Christ. Each local church was autonomous, and would gather its members to seek God together to discern his will. When they met, they held that God could speak through anyone present—not just those who led the meeting. So they listened well to one another.

ALEX: So does this continue in Baptist churches today?

STEVE: Yes, the autonomy of each local Baptist church is a key characteristic of our life together, and we gather regularly, as the early Baptists did, to discern God's will.

ALEX: What happens when you disagree? How do you sort that out?

STEVE: We talk things through and we pray together. In this way we try to reach a consensus, moving to a vote when we need to.

ALEX: It all sounds very egalitarian and democratic.

STEVE: Yes, but I must emphasise that the aim is not to win an argument, but to work out together what God would have us do. It is sometimes called 'discerning the mind of Christ'. In my experience there is nothing quite like it—some of the best and most memorable moments of church life have been in meetings where a tricky issue has been navigated by members joining together in prayer and taking time to share what each one senses of God's will.

ALEX: So is your working group part of this approach?

STEVE: Absolutely, yes. That is our understanding of what we are doing—joining together as followers of Christ to navigate a difficult issue, seeking God's wisdom as we do so. Worship and prayer will be an important aspect of what we do, since we are looking to God to lead us into truth and love. My favourite definition of this process is 'figuring out what to do together with the help of the Holy Spirit'[4]— which really says it like it is. Some refer to it as 'theological reflection', and there are various models that have been devised to lead people in a conversation that is open to God's leading: the simplest being to start with a situation or an issue, to articulate and explore its dimensions together, and then to draw upon the resources of our faith in order to arrive at some kind of proposed action. There are much more complex models, but that is the essence of it. In secular research methodology, it resembles a discipline sometimes referred to as 'action research'. One Christian researcher has coined the phrase 'theological action research'...[5] (*Steve suddenly notices that Alex is looking tired*)—oh dear, too much information?

ALEX: (*Yawning*) Maybe just a little.

STEVE: My apologies!

STEVE: (*Draining his coffee cup*) Shall we make a move then, my friend?

ALEX: Yes, though there was one more question in my mind.

STEVE: Let me have it.

ALEX: Well, I understand that the working group has been commissioned by the members of the church to do some... theological reflection, was it?

STEVE: Yes.

ALEX: And at some point the group will report back to the

members, who will then presumably do some more reflecting, and make some kind of decision or take a position on the issue of same-sex partnerships.

STEVE: You have it.

ALEX: So, given the autonomy of Baptist churches, am I right in thinking that whatever outcomes there might be will really only be applicable to your particular church community and those who might join you?

STEVE: Yes and no. Yes, we will have arrived at our discernment as a local church, and it will be our response to the issue. However, although autonomous, Baptist churches believe in association—at local, national, and international levels. We are part of a Union (The Baptist Union of Great Britain), which employs staff to give some broader leadership to our churches, and we have a council that meets to seek God for the movement as a whole (essentially the same process of discernment practiced at the local level) giving guidance in matters that concern us all.

ALEX: So, it appears you do have an authority structure after all? Do you have Bishops?

STEVE: We have Regional Ministers, who advise and support local ministers, but it remains a firm principle that each local church has the liberty (and I would add responsibility) to interpret the way of Christ—the One who we worship as God and seek to obey. This is roughly what is stated in the first Declaration of Principle of our Union. I can send you the exact wording if you are interested.

ALEX: Okay, but back to my original question—will the outcomes of your local church decision on same sex relationships have any bearing beyond your own community?

STEVE: I hope so. I would venture that it has the potential to inform and influence other Baptist churches that are grappling with the same issue—not just the outcome but also the process followed.

ALEX: Just Baptist churches?

STEVE: Well, no. This is an issue that all churches in all traditions are wrestling with. So I hope my work will have value beyond the Baptist family. Again, the process as much as any outcomes.

ALEX: What about those who don't follow Jesus but care about the issue?

STEVE: Again, I hope so—I'd like to find a way to make this work accessible beyond the church.

ALEX: Enough questions. I hope your first session goes well.

STEVE: Thanks, Alex—you're a star.

EMAIL FROM STEVE TO ALEX

Sent at 19:04 later the same day

Hi Alex,

I really enjoyed our chat at the Goose today.

The First Declaration of Principle of the Baptist Union of Great Britain is

That our Lord and Saviour Jesus Christ, God manifest in the flesh, is the sole and absolute authority in all matters pertaining to faith and practice, as revealed in the Holy Scriptures, and that each church has liberty, under the guidance of the Holy Spirit, to interpret and administer His laws. [6]

For me, this statement is crucial to what we are doing, for it holds together an uncompromising commitment to Jesus Christ as Lord (and the Scriptures that reveal Him), with the liberty (and responsibility I believe) of each church to work out what it means to follow in His ways.

Have a good evening, Alex—I look forward to catching up again soon.

Steve

Two things to note about what follows…

1. The reports on the working group sessions do not give the full details of our interactions, but rather the gist of our conversations—captured by myself and checked back with the group after each session.

2. The names of those involved in the working group have all been changed except for my own. Likewise, I have not used the real names of those who have told me their stories for inclusion in this work.

CHAPTER 4

First Gathering (Session One)

Church Youth Lounge: Saturday, 15 February 2014—9:00 to 13:00

Present: Steve, Greta, Richard, Lewis, Chris, Maureen, Abigail, Patrick, James and Dru
Absent: Erica and Monica

The first meeting of the group was a whole morning together. The purpose of this session was to allow Steve to take the group through the Baptist Union materials, 'Baptists Exploring Issues of Homosexuality'[1], as a way into the conversation and to help us get our bearings for the months ahead.

After a short time of worship, we took time to introduce ourselves and to share how we were each feeling. A number within the group spoke of feeling 'torn': desiring to welcome and include those who are homosexual without judging, and yet anxious that the Bible's teaching on same-sex behaviour did not seem to allow this. Some spoke of a 'head and heart' divergence—usually meaning that their head said 'no', following the biblical prohibitions, while their heart said 'yes' to being inclusive. A good number expressed the sense of relief and liberation at being able to talk about a subject that is often avoided in church.

Steve went on to remind everyone of the task we were taking on together: *to craft a pastoral response to those who live with same-sex desires and seek to follow Christ*, to be submitted to the church meeting in July of 2014. He then set out a proposed approach to the task. Essentially, Steve called the group to a conversation that befits our shared commitment to follow Christ and reflecting our Baptist heritage. This was to include a commitment to the Christian Scriptures as our primary text, depending on the Holy Spirit to guide us into truth—as articulated in the first principle of the Baptist Union.[2] We took some time to get the measure of this statement and to consider how we might enact it in our conversation together. This involved a discussion of what constituted a good theological conversation, including attention to what might be termed our 'Big Story'—moving from Creation to Fall to Redemption to New Creation.[3] It also included the key theological question, 'What kind of God does Scripture reveal?'—recognising that our answers to this question will significantly shape our understanding of what it means to live faithfully towards Him. We agreed upon complimentary approaches to listening to what Scripture is saying to us today: sometimes working from the text to the world; while at other times the other way around. The group also agreed on some principles concerning the integrity and quality of our interactions: such as being aware of how we are shaped by our own individual backgrounds, as well as the culture we share. We agreed upon practicing mutual respect, seeking to listen well and, above all, letting love inform and guide our conversation.

Having agreed these general principles, the group decided upon the following specific protocols:

- We are aiming for a space to explore ideas and feelings without fear of being judged. Sometimes one or other may want to try out an idea that is tentative, and we want to encourage this.
- We desire for the group to be supportive of one another—sometimes it might be helpful for one of us to seek out another group member to talk over how the conversations we are having are impacting them.
- We are free to share our own views with others outside the group (being wise) but not the views of other group members.
- It's fine to talk with others (outside the group) about how the group is getting on in general terms—bearing in mind that they will

not have the same support we have in working these issues through (be wise and caring).

Having reached agreements on the approach of our conversation and some specific protocols, we proceeded to the materials provided by the Baptist Union (BU) working group.

SCIENCE, STATISTICS AND THE SPIRIT OF THE AGE

Steve gave a brief overview of the various kinds of research into the causes of homosexuality.[4] He reported that overall the scientific community leans towards genetic causation, but recognises to varying degrees the impact of environmental factors and life-style choices on genetic dispositions.[5] He offered a caution against the danger of oversimplifications: such as the erroneous idea that there is a 'gay-gene'[6] that determines that some people are homosexual, or the 'one size fits all' approach that views all incidences of same-sex attraction as arising from some kind of deficit in relationships with mothers or fathers.[7]

The group found the materials both stimulating and perplexing. There was no clear conclusion to be reached on causation, except the likelihood of a combination of genetic disposition, environmental factors and personal choice in determining sexual orientation, identity and lifestyle. However, it did occur to the group that whatever the balance of factors at play, it was important to recognise that a small minority of people experience same-sex attraction as a 'given', with little likelihood of change. So that perhaps the most pertinent issue is not causation, but how we respond to people as they are.

FOCUS: ON CAUSATION AND CHANGE

Those who have reviewed the various studies looking into the causes of homosexuality have tended to arrive at what might be called 'integrative theories'. Keener and Swartzendruber, for example, conclude, 'It is impossible to neatly separate our heredity from our environment; both are important determinants in the person we have become.'[8] Jones and Yarhouse concur with this, and have reflected helpfully on the popular assumptions that genetic causation is firmly established and psychological studies largely discredited.[9] On the basis of their investigations, they assert that biological theories are far from conclusive and that psychological theories are far from being disproved.[10] A much more recent report has made even stronger assertions against the assumption of genetic causation, stating that 'The understanding of sexual orientation as an innate, biological fixed property of human beings—the idea that people are "born that way"—is not supported by scientific evidence.'[11] The writers go on to say that 'While there is evidence that biological factors such as genes and hormones are associated with sexual behaviours and attractions, there are no compelling causal biological explanations for human sexual orientation.'[12]

Leanne Payne is among those who has championed psychological causation in her therapeutic approach to helping people find freedom from homosexual desires—viewing these as symptoms of broken relationships. In her book 'Broken Image' she asserts that, 'In spite of reports to the contrary, there is no real scientific evidence that genetic or endocrine factors are causative in homosexual behaviour.'[13] Payne goes on to open her case-book to show how prayerful attention to relationship deficits in the personal development of an individual—such as that caused by an absent or emotionally distant father—can enable a person to find healing from a distorted sexuality.[14]

In his book, 'Exchanging the Truth of God for a Lie', Jeremy Marks cites Leanne Payne as one of the inspirations for the ministry of 'Courage'[15], an organisation set up by Marks in February 1988 to offer support to those living with same-sex desires to live celibate lives and, as the ministry developed in confidence, to move on from homosexual orientation. In his book, Marks describes how the ministry initially burgeoned, moving from weekly support groups to the provision of a one-year residential discipleship course that provided a strong community life as a context for overcoming homosexual desires. However, there came a point when Marks began to feel uneasy and unsure about the long term fruit of the ministry as he discovered that an alarming number of former community members did not continue to experience the freedom they had found in the community, with many becoming depressed or finding a greater sense of release and freedom in actually accepting their homosexual orientation. Shaken by the seeming ineffectiveness of the healing ministry for those who were homosexual, and the apparent ill-effects of insisting on celibacy for those who could not change, Marks led an 'about-turn'[16] and committed *Courage* to supporting gay Christians in their life-style choices, whether that be celibacy, a committed, loving (sexual) relationship with someone of the same sex, or continuing within a gay/straight marriage.

Jones and Yarhouse, made a thorough appraisal of a range of scientific studies into the success rates of change therapies, most of which were carried out in the 1950s, 1960s and 1970s. They comment that most of these were methodologically weak— particularly in the way outcomes were measured—to the extent that their results are usually deemed unreliable. However, looking across a wide range of studies, Jones and Yarhouse offer an average positive outcome (changes in thinking, behaviour and perhaps orientation) of 33%'[17] It is important to note that this estimate includes a range of behaviour modifications and impulse changes that do not constitute a change of orientation. It appears that while there may be some evidence of radical change, it is rare.[18]

Group Session One Continued

Following the brief tour of scientific investigations into causation and change, the working group considered sociological research into the statistical incidence of same-sex orientation and behaviour. This began with the famous work of Alfred Kinsey, carried out in the 1940s and 1950s, which was built on the idea of sexual experience as a continuum ranging from exclusively heterosexual to exclusively homosexual, with all gradations in between. (It was Kinsey's work that gave us the familiar and often quoted '1 in 10' statistic for male homosexuality.) Steve referred to more recent studies, such as the first National Survey of Sexual Attitudes and Lifestyles (Natsal 1), 1990, which reported that around 1% of men and 0.5% of women were same-sex attracted, with the percentage for actual sexual experience being the same for men and a little lower (0.3%) for women. [19] These results came as something of surprise for most members of the group.

The disparity between Kinsey's '1 in 10' and the more recent statistics led us to consider the highly politicised nature of the same-sex issue and the lack of nuance given in media portrayals of viewpoints held. The point was made that those who hold a view that is not wholly accepting of the choices made by those who live with same-sex desires can easily be branded 'homo-phobic', even when the middle ground is held with careful thought and compassion. We agreed that part of our task was to resist such pressure, along with the pressure from the other end of the spectrum, where even entering into such a conversation as ours might be considered an act of unfaithfulness regarding what the Bible clearly states (i.e. that homosexuality is to be roundly condemned).

FOCUS: ON MEASURING SEXUALITY

The Natsal 1 survey referenced above is over twenty years old. Understandably the group were keen to learn if more recent studies showed significant change. A much more recent survey conducted for the Office of National Statistics between January and December of 2012 indicated percentages of men and women identifying as gay or lesbian at 1.5% and 0.7% respectively—suggesting little change over two decades.[20] Newspapers reporting on these results, including the Guardian and the Daily Mail, reflected on the disparity between Kinsey's '1 in 10' and the ONS data, and rehearsed the usual criticisms of Kinsey's methods—such as the non-random selection of interviewees—but went on to question whether persistent taboos around sexual identity continue to inhibit disclosure of sexual orientation. Supporting this suspicion, Rose Everleth, writing for the Smithsonian, reports on a new study in America that has returned higher proportions than usual of those identifying as gay or lesbian, and observes that this seems to be due to the use of 'veiled' questions.[21]

Whether or not the proportions of those identifying as gay or lesbian are understated, they hardly tell the whole story of sexual diversity in Britain, or indeed America. This can be demonstrated by looking at some other measures of sexuality reported in the Natsal surveys of 1990, 2000 and 2010, as shown in the table below.

Sexual practices with partners of the same sex[22]	Men			Women		
	Natsal 1	*Natsal 2*	*Natsal 3*	*Natsal 1*	*Natsal 2*	*Natsal 3*
Any sexual experience or contact with partner of the same sex	6.0%	8.4%	7.3%	3.7%	9.7%	16.0%
Any sexual experience with genital contact with partner of the same sex	3.6%	5.4%	4.8%	1.8%	4.0%	7.9%
At least one sexual partner of the same sex in the past 5 years	1.5%	2.5%	2.9%	0.8%	2.4%	4.7%

These percentages clearly show that beyond those who identify as gay, lesbian or bi-sexual, there are considerably more who disclose some degree of same-sex experience, with the overall trend from Natsal 1 to Natsal 3 being upward. A closer look at the Natsal 3 statistics reveals a higher level of same-sex sexual activity among younger age-groups and a more fluid sexuality among females—the last point strikingly indicated in the grid above with 16% of women reporting some kind of same-sex contact or experience.

It is helpful in the face of such data to recognise and distinguish between those who are exclusively or predominantly homosexual in orientation and those whose sexuality is less certain or more fluid who are engaged in same-sex behaviours of various kinds. Where such behaviours move beyond commitment and faithfulness, we might see a more obvious application of the so called condemning texts, than for those of pronounced homosexual orientation who live in faithful, long term relationships. This will clearly depend on how these texts are interpreted: whether they are aimed only at sexual behaviour that is lustful, exploitative, experimental, and divorced from long-term loving relationship—or if they have a wider reference.

To these texts and the wider perspective of the Bible, the working group turned its attention to next.

JOIN THE CONVERSATION...

Here is the second opportunity within this work to pause and reflect, either as an individual reader or in a group context.

1 What are your thoughts and feelings about what you have read? It may help you to write them down. If you are in a group context, take time to let each person share, listening carefully to one another.

2 Investigations into the causes of same-sex attraction can prove complicated and bewildering. If there is a minority of the population who experience same-sex attraction as a 'given', how important is it really to determine whether biological or developmental factors are more or less influential?

3 When considering their response to same-sex relationships, a number of group members spoke of 'head and heart divergence'. Can you identify with this? What does your head say and what does your heart say about this issue?

4 At the heart of being Baptist is an utter commitment to the Lordship of Christ and a conviction that we need to work out (discern) together what this means in practice (p. 42). How might this help us in tackling an issue over which we disagree? How is it possible for Christians to look to the same Scriptures and rely upon the same Spirit to guide them, and yet come to different conclusions?

5 Do you agree that there is little room for nuance in discussions about same-sex relationships in our/your society?

6 What is your reaction to the statistics on those who identify as homosexual in their orientation and behaviour (pp. 50-52)?

7 Take another look at the table in the focus piece 'On Measuring Sexuality' (p. 52). How do you react to the suggestion that the Bible may bear a different message to those who are 'fluid' or experimental in expressing their sexuality, compared to those in loving, stable same-sex relationships? This may be a question to revisit after the next chapter.

CHAPTER 5

What the Bible Has to Say

GROUP SESSION ONE CONTINUED

Before looking together at the texts that make reference to same-sex behaviour, Steve proposed some preliminary agreements (shared understandings of the biblical perspective on human sexuality and its expression) on which we might build our discussions:

- Promiscuous and exploitative sex is wrong—whether homosexual or heterosexual.

- Scripture affirms marriage between male and female as the creational intention/norm.

- God is a God of Covenant relationship, reflected in loving, faithful relationships: including marriage, friendship, the care of children, etc.

The group had no difficulty in agreeing to these and also confirmed that the question before us was not about whether any kind of same-sex behaviour might be acceptable, but specifically that within a loving, committed, life partnership between two people of the same sex.

From here, a few more points were offered and agreed relating to the specific texts to be considered:

- There are few texts that deal directly with homosexuality and all of them are disapproving.

- In the ancient world there was no distinction between 'sexual orientation' and 'sexual practice'.

- A key question is whether these texts address all homosexual behaviour or certain forms prevalent in the ancient world, e.g., pederasty.

The first of these was accepted as self-evident. The second was received as helpful in avoiding the projection of this relatively modern way of thinking onto the ancient text. The third was to become a familiar friend, for in all our discussions of the *condemning texts* we kept coming back to the question: 'What is being addressed here?'

So our first consideration (as a working group) of our key-texts began. We read them together, and Steve outlined both traditional and revisionist understandings of each text to provoke and facilitate the discussion. This took the remainder of our time—so that we had to agree at the end to pick up the other main session envisaged (responding to stories) at our next meeting.

By the end of our time, the pertinence of the key question (what is being forbidden and condemned?) was clear to everyone, and it was also clear that the group held a range of positions on this, as might be expected from the way the group was set up. Some expressed the conviction that the texts were referring to certain categories of same-sex behaviour, including abusive (gang rape, prostitution and pederasty), perverse (deviating from natural inclination) and cultic (temple ritual) forms, and that the morality of a loving, committed same-sex partnership is not in view at all. Some held that at least some of the references seem to speak to same-sex behaviour across the board—such as the reference in Romans 1 to that which is 'natural' and 'unnatural'[1]—and felt that the traditional interpretations of these passages were to be held with due respect until evidence to the contrary was compelling. Others felt unsure—challenged by the revisionist views but not wholly convinced.

FOCUS: ON THE 'CONDEMNING TEXTS'

There are seven passages in the Bible that refer directly to same-sex erotic behaviours.

GENESIS 19:1–13

The two angels arrived at Sodom in the evening, and Lot was sitting in the gateway of the city. When he saw them, he got up to meet them and bowed down with his face to the ground. 'My lords,' he said, 'please turn aside to your servant's house. You can wash your feet and spend the night and then go on your way early in the morning.' 'No,' they answered, 'we will spend the night in the square.' But he insisted so strongly that they did go with him and entered his house. He prepared a meal for them, baking bread without yeast, and they ate.

Before they had gone to bed, all the men from every part of the city of Sodom—both young and old—surrounded the house. They called to Lot, 'Where are the men who came to you tonight? Bring them out to us so that we can have sex with them.' Lot went outside to meet them and shut the door behind him and said, 'No, my friends. Don't do this wicked thing. Look, I have two daughters who have never slept with a man. Let me bring them out to you, and you can do what you like with them. But don't do anything to these men, for they have come under the protection of my roof.' 'Get out of our way,' they replied. 'This fellow came here as a foreigner, and now he wants to play the judge! We'll treat you worse than them.' They kept bringing pressure on Lot and moved forward to break down the door. But the men inside reached out and pulled Lot back into the house and shut the door. Then they struck the men who were at the door of the house, young and old, with blindness so that they could not find the door.

The two men said to Lot, 'Do you have anyone else here—sons-in-law, sons or daughters, or anyone else in the city who belongs to you? Get them out of here, because we are going to destroy this place. The outcry of the Lord against its people is so great that he has sent us to destroy it.'

The story of Sodom and Gomorrah is deeply shocking to read, with the most shocking detail for modern ears being Lot's offer of his daughters to a marauding crowd (all men) who are intent on forcing themselves sexually on his male visitors (Genesis 19: 6–8). There is a story in the book of Judges (19:1–30) that bears many similarities to this one, in which a crowd of men demand that a traveller is brought out to them that they might 'know him' (19:22), and women are offered for sexual gratification to divert them from their intentions (19:23–24).[2]

There are numerous discussions among biblical commentators concerning what is to be understood from Lot's appeal to the men who are banging at his door, 'Don't do this wicked thing' (v. 7). For while it may seem obvious to the modern reader (the threat of sexual violence), it is often pointed out that the offensiveness of the threatened action may lie in a breach of hospitality, for it was a near sacred duty within Lot's cultural setting to protect and care for those who came under one's roof. [3] This does not take away, of course, the violent and ugly nature of the actions threatened, but it may give pause to locating the strength of Lot's appeal in a revulsion to the homosexual act per se—rather, it is likely to be the violent abuse of guests that is the 'wicked thing'. While the homosexual act is popularly associated with Sodom and Gomorrah (the word Sodomy being derived from Sodom), other Old Testament references point to the sins of injustice, pride, greed and a neglect of the poor[4]—a combination that Walter Brueggemann sums up as a 'general disorder of a society organised against God'.[5]

What are we to make of these harrowing tales, and what bearing might they have on the modern issue of same-sex relationships? Referring to the story of Sodom and Gomorrah, Richard Hays states boldly that it is simply 'irrelevant to the topic (of same-sex consensual relationships)'.[6] Many other traditionalists would agree—the threat of gang rape, aimed at men and carried out (in one case) on a woman, surely has no bearing on how we regard those who live in loving, committed, same-sex relationships. Our discussion on this passage might easily end there. However, Brownson, while agreeing with

Hays, suggests that the two stories might throw some light on the antipathy shown elsewhere in the Bible to sexual relations between men.[7] Brownson is keen to point out the 'limited moral vision' inherent in the stories, in which the rape of a woman is considered less heinous than the rape of a man. He argues that this expresses a strong patriarchal outlook in which women hold a much lower status to men, which, in turn, helps to explain why a same-sex act would have been so offensive to ancients—since it put a man into the role or place of a woman, thus reducing him to a lower status. These are themes worth keeping in mind as we move to the other 'condemning passages'.

LEVITICUS 18:22 AND 20:13

Do not have sexual relations with a man as one does with a woman; that is detestable… If a man has sexual relations with a man as one does with a woman, both of them have done what is detestable. They are to be put to death; their blood will be on their own heads.

These verses are part of the holiness code that is part of the Covenant of Yahweh with Israel. The code expresses in detail what it means for Israel to be set apart to God and distinctive in the world. As Gordon Fee has reminded us, this is not our (Gentile believers) covenant and we are under no obligation to obey its stipulations except where they are renewed in the New Covenant.[8] Yet, we understand that the code has value for us in revealing God's character and what it means for us to live as his people, so long as we recognise its cultural setting and seek to discern between enduring principles and their cultural expressions. Most see in the law code a mix of ethical and ritual laws, and it is easy to spot the stipulations we have deemed unnecessary to fulfil in our day—including regulations about cutting hair (19:27), wearing mixed fabrics (19:19) and what to plant in one's field (19:19). Many of the stipulations do have a moral feel to them—including those concerning sexual relations. Bestiality, incest and adultery are all prohibited, along with 'having sexual relations with a man as one does with a woman' (18:22 and 20:13), which is declared to be 'detestable', warranting the death penalty for both men involved.

Hays states that this prohibition is unambiguous and 'stands as the foundation for the subsequent universal rejection of male same-sex intercourse within Judaism.'[9] Yet he adds that its relevance for Christian ethics can only be decided by looking at how the New Testament writers treated it—that is, did they affirm it or leave it behind?

Others have not been content to simply feel the clarity and force of the prohibition against male same-sex behaviour, and have sought to penetrate the moral logic behind it. There are three aspects frequently explored.

Firstly, it is observed that one rationale of the law code was to keep God's people from imitating the practices of those around them (see 20:23–24). Brownson points out that the word translated 'detestable' or 'abomination' is closely linked to idolatrous practices in at least thirty-nine other passages in Scripture.[10] On the strength of this, the IVP New Bible Dictionary takes the view that the prohibitions against male-to-male sex in Leviticus, understood in context, are aimed primarily at idolatrous practices, and are not necessarily to be given wider application.[11] Secondly, concerns with procreation are detected in the text, leading to the idea that homosexual behaviour might be seen negatively because it cannot lead to childbirth. Thirdly, there is Brownson's contention that the prohibitions are essentially about male honour in a patriarchal society, where a male taking a female role and being penetrated by another male would have been considered disgraceful, due to the status of the male being acted upon being lowered to that of a woman. Again, if Brownson is right, this might also explain why there is no female-to-female equivalent (as there is for bestiality (20:15–16)), since 'there is no such degradation operative in these cases'.[12]

The upshot of these points, either separately or in combination, is the assertion that the prohibitions in the text have a limited reference, either to the sexual conduct around pagan temple worship and/or to the particular values and sensibilities of the patriarchal society to which they were addressed. Thus, it might be argued that we cannot read them as timeless ordinances. Many would disagree with this assertion, countering that the moral logic underlying them is not exhausted by cultic associations or particular cultural forms, and would agree with Hays that we need to turn to the New Testament to see what decisions are made there about the relevance of these moral commands to Christian ethics.

1 CORINTHIANS 6:9–10

Or do you not know that wrongdoers will not inherit the kingdom of God? Do not be deceived: neither the sexually immoral nor idolaters nor adulterers nor male prostitutes nor practising homosexuals nor thieves nor the greedy nor drunkards nor slanderers nor swindlers will inherit the kingdom of God.

In 1 Corinthians, Paul writes to a community that it seems had begun to think their spiritual life in Christ made it unimportant what they did with their bodies (6:18–20). 'Do not be deceived,' says Paul, 'neither the sexually immoral nor idolaters nor adulterers nor male prostitutes nor practising homosexuals... will inherit the kingdom God' (6:9,10). Now the Greek words translated 'male prostitutes' and 'practising homosexuals' in the TNIV are *malakoi* (denoting 'soft' or 'feminine') and *arsenokoitai* (literally 'sleepers with men' or 'men-bedders'). It is important to realise that neither of these are technical terms meaning 'homosexuals', since no such word exists in Hebrew, nor was there such a concept of human identity in the ancient world. *Malakoi* was used in Hellenistic Greek as pejorative slang to describe the 'passive' partners—often young boys—in same-sex erotic activity. *Arsenokoitai* is not found in any extra-biblical sources earlier than 1 Corinthians, yet its literal meaning and its proximity to *malakoi* in the list has suggested to some that it refers to the active partner in pederasty. Reflecting on the placement of the two words in Paul's list, Jerome Murphy O' Connor writes:

> At first sight these do not seem to fit with the other vices because sometimes homosexual relationships are models of enduring affection. In reality, however, the terms suggest an effeminate call-boy who is used by an older sodomite. This was the most common form of homosexuality in the ancient world, and was viciously exploited on both sides. Thus for Paul it typified the degenerate relationships that characterised society. [13]

In his discussion of *arsenokoitai*, Hays cites the work of Robin Scroggs who has shown that the word is a translation of the Hebrew *mishkav zakur* ('lying with a male') derived directly from Leviticus 18:22 and 20:13.[14] Hays underlines the importance of this connection, asserting that it demonstrates an affirmation by the apostle Paul of the longstanding negative assessment of male same-sex erotic behaviour, which thereby continues to be valid in the New Testament era.[15]

Hays' point is convincingly made, yet this hardly establishes *arsenokoitai* as a blanket term for any form of homosexual behaviour. In the context, it most likely points to well-known and common practices in the day, including male prostitution, sexual rituals in the pagan temples, and pederasty—the latter being widespread in the ancient Grecian and Roman world, and a pastoral issue within churches whose membership included slaves, many of whom would have been the passive partners in such arrangements.[16]

1 TIMOTHY 1:9–10A

We also know that the law is made not for the righteous but for lawbreakers and rebels, the ungodly and sinful, the unholy and irreligious, for those who kill their fathers or mothers, for murderers, for the sexually immoral, for those practising homosexuality, for slave traders and liars and perjurers.

In 1 Timothy 1:10 we find another vice-list including *arsenokoitai*. While *malakoi* is not present, two other words *pornoi* ('fornicators' or possibly 'male prostitutes') and *andropodistai* ('slave dealers' or 'kidnappers') might, in combination refer to a particularly sordid arrangement: namely 'slave dealers acting as pimps for their captured and castrated boys servicing the *arsenokoitai*, the men who made use of them.'[17] Such practices have a modern equivalent in people trafficking, which is surely just as deserving of inclusion in Paul's vice-list, alongside those who murder their parents, murderers, liars and perjurers. Whereas, it seems incongruent to place loving, same-sex partnerships in the same list, which is effectively what we do if *arsenokoitai* is made a reference to all forms of homosexual behaviour. This would seem to be a category error. We cannot of course know for certain what was in the mind of Paul when he wrote what he did. It is likely, as Timothy Keller argues, that 'as a cultured and travelled Roman Citizen, Paul would have been very familiar with long-term, stable, loving relationships between same-sex couples.'[18] Yet the language and tone used by Paul does not seem to point us in this direction, but rather to the kind of relationships where one man dominated another sexually and others made a profit from it.

ROMANS 1:18–32

The wrath of God is being revealed from heaven against all the godlessness and wickedness of human beings who suppress the truth by their wickedness, since what may be known about God is plain to them, because God has made it plain to them. For since the creation of the world God's invisible qualities—his eternal power and divine nature—have been clearly seen, being understood from what has been made, so that people are without excuse.

For although they knew God, they neither glorified him as God nor gave thanks to him, but their thinking became futile and their foolish hearts were darkened. Although they claimed to be wise, they became fools and exchanged the glory of the immortal God for images made to look like mortal human beings and birds and animals and reptiles.

Therefore God gave them over in the sinful desires of their hearts to sexual impurity for the degrading of their bodies with one another. They exchanged the truth about God for a lie, and worshipped and served created things rather than the Creator—who is for ever praised, Amen.

Because of this, God gave them over to shameful lusts. Even their women exchanged natural sexual relations for unnatural ones. In the same way the men also abandoned natural relations with women and were inflamed with lust for one another. Men committed shameful acts with other men, and received in themselves the due penalty for their error.

Furthermore, just as they did not think it worthwhile to retain the knowledge of God, so God gave them over to a depraved mind, so that they do what ought not to be done. They have become filled with every kind of wickedness, evil, greed and depravity. They are full of envy, murder, strife, deceit and malice. They are gossips, slanderers, God-haters, insolent, arrogant and boastful; they invent ways of doing evil; they disobey their parents; they have no understanding, no fidelity, no love, no mercy. Although they know God's righteous decree that those who do such things deserve death, they not only continue to do these very things but also approve of those who practise them.

At an early stage in his articulation of the gospel in the book of Romans, Paul launches into a polemic against the wickedness of the pagan (non-Jewish) world that would have been quite familiar to his Jewish readers: just the kind of rhetoric that other Jewish writers and Stoic Philosophers engaged in at the time. The essential approach of all such denouncements was to trace all the sinful and destructive features of society to idolatry: to worshipping created things rather than the creator. In Paul's handling, the consequences of this fundamental sin are played out progressively in those who, having exchanged the truth of God for a lie, give themselves to shameful and degrading sexual acts.

Because of this, God gave them over to shameful lusts. Even their women exchanged natural relations for unnatural ones. In the same way the men also abandoned natural relations with women and were inflamed with lust for one another. Men committed shameful acts with other men, and received in themselves the due penalty for their error.[19]

James Alison has reflected on this process, from idolatry through deception to degradation, and has posited that it is framed entirely within the context of pagan worship.[20] Thus, for Alison, references to 'unnatural' sexual behaviour point to the frenzied sexual antics that went on in and around the pagan temples throughout the Mediterranean world in Paul's day. Alison cites the cults of Cybele, Atys and Aphrodite, whose largest temple was in Corinth where Paul most probably wrote his letter to Rome, and describes rites that involved cross-dressing and orgiastic frenzies in which men allowed themselves to be penetrated, often culminating in some men castrating themselves and becoming eunuchs.

Alison's analysis is worthy of consideration, given that the heart of Paul's diagnosis of sinful humankind is misplaced worship. If he is right, then the reference to same-sex behaviour is quite specific and would have little bearing on loving, same-sex relationships today. However, it seems likely that Paul's intended reference was wider than this—including at least the common practices of male-prostitution and pederasty, as described in the discussion of the 'vice-lists' above, for these can just as easily be seen as outcomes of misplaced worship, and concord with the out of control, lust-driven sexual behaviour portrayed in the passage. The question—as with the other texts discussed above—is whether we can legitimately extend these denouncements to loving, same-sex relationships.

Richard Hays is among those who see deeper implications in the text. He argues that Paul's depiction of the pagan world turning from worshipping the Creator to images of created things would certainly have evoked the Creation narrative for his Jewish readers. Hays argues that they would have seen the abandonment of God-ordained gender roles through unnatural sexual behaviour as a clear sign of rebellion—'a sacrament (so to speak) of the anti-religion of human beings who refuse to honour God as Creator [...] an outward and visible sign of an inward and spiritual reality—the rejection of the Creator's design.'[21]

Brownson takes issue with Hays (and most traditionalists) regarding the assumption that biological complementarity is at the heart of the image of God in humankind, arguing that the language of 'one-flesh' is best understood as the creation of a new kinship group, rather than the joining of two halves to make a whole. Offering a thorough study of the key terms and themes in Genesis 2, and pursuing their use and development in other parts of the Bible, he concludes that biological complementarity has been overstated as the rationale for understanding what is at the heart of the bond of marriage.[22] Brownson concedes that the biblical writers would have assumed that marriage as a kinship bond was naturally between a man and a woman, and that the Bible as a whole does not envisage any other pattern (i.e., same-sex kinship bonds)—yet asserts that the idea of marriage as a kinship bond is not necessarily at odds with a loving, committed same-sex union.

The main point of contention between traditionalists and revisionists in Romans 1 is the meaning of the Greek word *physis* ('nature'). Traditionalists understand the term, in Paul's use and in extra-biblical literature, to mean the natural order of creation—that is, what God has designed and purposed in creation—including the biological complementarity of male and female. In Hellenistic Judaism, the God-given order, manifest in Creation, was considered to be perfectly aligned with the Law of Moses. Some revisionists have offered the alternative interpretation of *physis* as what is *natural to each individual,* implying that what Paul is addressing in Romans 1:26–27 is perversion (people moving against their natural orientation) and so cannot be applied to those whose orientation is homosexual. Hays objects that this is to 'lapse into anachronism', since the notion of 'orientation' was not in the ancient mindset.[23] He is surely right in this. However, Brownson has countered by asserting that while there was no concept of a different sexual orientation, the ancients did have a sense of what was natural to the individual, which was for a man to desire a woman and to unite with her in marriage for procreation. Brownson argues that this was one strand in a three-stranded understanding of what was 'natural' (or according to nature). Firstly, there was personal disposition (with no conception of same-sex orientation); secondly there was the created order; and thirdly there was social convention. The last of these might be illustrated by Paul's contention elsewhere that it is 'against nature' for a man to wear his hair long, which cannot be read easily as an appeal to the created order (1 Corinthians 11:14). Brownson refers to this text, and goes on to argue that social convention is also implicit in Paul's reference to what is natural in Romans: including a patriarchal outlook that placed women below men and would have viewed a male-male sexual act as the degrading of the passive partner since it lowered his status to that of a woman (as discussed above). For Brownson, the convergence of personal, communal and cosmic aspects in determining what is 'natural' enables people to work out what it means to live well (that is, in God's way) in the world—and this convergence, he argues, will not be the same for us in the twentieth century as it was for the first century church. Thus, our less patriarchal more egalitarian culture, and our understanding of sexuality, as informed by the scientific studies referenced earlier, will lead us to a different sense of what it means to live according 'nature', that is, to live in God's way.

Brownson has put up some good arguments for a revised reading of Romans 1, backed by thorough investigation of the biblical text, and has given a credible challenge to the traditionalist view on same-sex unions. This by no means decides the matter, and this discussion only really scratches the surface of the debate. Yet enough has been indicated in relation to Romans 1 and to the other condemning texts here to venture to conclude that both traditionalist and revisionist readings are tenable within a conversation premised on a high view of Scripture. In particular, it is reasonable to take the view that the condemning texts refer to particular forms of same-sex erotic behaviour and have no bearing on the loving, same-sex unions about which we are concerned, though equally reasonable to see a wider inference. In the end, the matter will not be decided within the limited territory of a handful of verses. We need to look beyond them to the whole witness of Scripture.

Join the Conversation…

Time to pause and reflect again…

1 What are your thoughts and feelings about what you have read? It may help you to write them down. If you are in a group context, take time to let each person share, listening carefully to one another.

2 How convincing do find the various challenges to the traditional interpretations of these passages?

3 Has anything in this chapter challenged your thinking?

4 Do you agree that the key question for each of these passages is to determine what is being addressed—whether all expressions of homosexuality or certain forms of it?

To take the discussion forward, we need to look beyond the seven passages considered here to the broader witness of Scripture (the Big Story). This is where we are headed next. Before that, however, Alex has a question or two about the trustworthiness of the Bible…

CHAPTER 6

A Lot of Trust in a Book With a Talking Snake

Wild Goose Coffee House: Wednesday, 10 March—the time is 11:00

The Wild Goose is full and bustling. Alex and Steve are deep in conversation.

ALEX: So, how can you be so confident in an ancient book?

STEVE: That's a big question.

ALEX: Well, you guys are pinning so much on it—it seems important to ask.

STEVE: Fair enough: well, you could say that it has proved itself over the centuries—since the time when this collection of writings was brought together...

ALEX: *(Interrupting)* And when was that exactly?

STEVE: The Bible, as we have it, came together through the deliberations of a series of church councils. The collection of books that we have was agreed by the end of the fourth century.[1]

ALEX: How did they decide what to include and what to leave out?

STEVE: There were various criteria, including matters of authorship, the acceptance of writings in the church at large, consistency with the central doctrines of the church, evidence of high ethical values...

ALEX: *(Interrupting)* I imagine these were hot debates. How do you know they got it right? Decisions by committees can get quite political, with all kinds of vested interests at play.

STEVE: It was certainly not a flawless process, and you are right about the politics.[2] Yet, the results have stood the test of time. The agreed collection of books—known as the Canon of Scripture—along with the ancient Creeds (statements of core Christian belief) undergird the great variety of Christian traditions that have developed, and provide the basis of unity between them. In the end, it is a matter of trust that the God who inspired these writings also oversaw the decisions about which books to include in the Bible.

ALEX: That's a huge amount of trust in a book with a talking snake.

STEVE: I'm sorry?

ALEX: Doesn't the Bible start off with a story about how the world was created in seven days, a naked couple in a paradise garden, and a talking snake?

STEVE: Well, yes, I suppose...

ALEX: *(Interrupting)* This is the book that you revere above all other knowledge, and it has a talking snake—not to mention a war god with a bad temper, who is not beyond giving the order to wipe out an entire people group![3]

STEVE: Now you're really getting down to it.

ALEX: Well I hope you don't just want me to nod politely at everything you say.

STEVE: No of course not, I was just a little taken aback by the passion with which you said all that.

ALEX: I surprised myself a bit! What about an answer or two? You can be passionate too, if you like!

STEVE: I'll see what I can do. I'll need to take you right back to the beginning, with the story of Creation…

ALEX: *(Interrupting)* Don't forget the snake!

STEVE: I won't. Let me start by saying that Christians have different ways of understanding the Creation story. Some take it very literally, holding that God created everything in seven days—even though the sun and moon were not created until day four (think about that). Others regard the seven days as seven ages or eras. Some Christians read the Creation narrative as a literal historical account, while others see it as a symbolic story—or maybe two symbolic stories—crafted to convey important truths, and are not so worried about it being literally true.

ALEX: What about evolution?

STEVE: Well, for those who take the opening chapters of the Bible as literal history, the theory of evolution has to be refuted, as it contradicts what they believe the Bible is teaching. I am thinking of Creationists who hold that the earth is young—thousands rather than billions of years old—and point to scientific research that they believe discredits a long evolutionary process. On the other hand, there are those who see no contradiction between evolutionary theory and the creation narrative in the Bible and view them as complementary.[4]

ALEX: So the Bible tells us that God created the world, and evolution tells us how it happened?

STEVE: As always, a much more concise version of my ramblings! Though I might add that the Bible tells us much more than 'God created'. The Creation Story—whether it's being understood as history or as a symbolic representation—is full of profound truths, truths that the theory of evolution cannot supply.

ALEX: Such as?

STEVE: Such as humankind being the crowning glory of God's creation.

ALEX: Huh! Well that's disputable, and even a bit arrogant, I think.

STEVE: Hold that thought. Let me carry on for a minute. The Creation Story tells us that God made us in His image—male and female. Made from the dust of the earth, yet bearing His image, and commissioned to rule over the rest of creation, to steward the earth.

ALEX: Well we didn't make a very good job of that!

STEVE: I agree with you, but that's where the second act comes in.

ALEX: I'm sorry?

STEVE: Imagine the Bible as a great literary drama split into four acts.

ALEX: Okay.

STEVE: **Act One: Creation**—God makes it all: earth and sky, rivers and lakes, every plant that springs from the earth; every creature that crawls, or climbs, or gallops, or glides; every vast mountain range; every intricate, beautiful, breath-taking detail (we'll leave aside the process and the timing for now). Crowning it all He makes humankind—fashioned from the dust. He breathes life into us— divine image-bearers; stewards of all creation. He stands back and admires His work and says, 'It's good—it's very good!'[5]

ALEX: You've told me that one already.

STEVE: Yes, I wanted to take a bit of a run up. **Act Two: The Fall of Humankind**—in which we rebel against the rule of God. We say 'no' to any kind of restriction or boundary to our freedom. We take life on our own terms.

ALEX: Is this where the apple and the talking snake come in?

STEVE: Yes, whether history or symbol, we witness the rebellion of humankind against our loving Creator.

ALEX: We strike out on our own!

STEVE: Yes, which is tragic because we were made for life-giving communion with the One who made us—God, the very source of our being.

ALEX: And the snake?

STEVE: The snake is the enemy of God and the enemy of humankind—inciting rebellion through insinuation: portraying every command of God as one more brick in our supposed captivity, a threat to our freedom.

ALEX: So are we talking about a red, horned devil with sulphurous breath and an arrow on the end of his tail?

STEVE: Would you prefer that to a talking snake?

ALEX: I'd prefer there wasn't any kind of devil at all—in fact, I think that such notions are rather laughable if I'm honest.

STEVE: Presumably you recognise the reality of evil…

IMPORTANT NOTE TO READER

Alex and Steve continue this conversation at quite some length, with Steve setting out the four Acts of the Biblical drama, and Alex continuing to push for an answer to his question about divinely sanctioned genocide in the Old Testament. What follows are **selected extracts** from this conversation that allow the four acts of the Biblical drama to be conveyed for the purpose of this work. If you would like to follow the whole conversation through, it is available as a short Kindle book, entitled *The Talking Snake and The Warrior God—A Wild Goose Encounter* by Stephen Elmes.

Please also note that apart from the stories of the Creation and the Fall, and some passages that refer to the rules of warfare in the Old Testament, I have not attempted to provide a full set of biblical references for this discussion, since it draws on so many of the biblical writings.

Extract 2

ALEX: So this is your view of the human condition?

STEVE: Not just the human condition, but also one shared with all of creation. We are broken image bearers, glorious creatures in captivity.

ALEX: Intriguing phrases.

STEVE: Yes, and for me, a profound description of life on earth that arises from Acts One and Two of the Biblical drama. For me, it fits with what I see in the world and how I experience life.

ALEX: How do you mean?

STEVE: I see such beauty, at times quite breath-taking—compelling evidence of a good Creation—and yet in so many ways it is spoilt or under threat. I see the image of God in others, and recognise it in myself, and yet I see the spoiling there too. We are broken, yet there are so many glimpses of lost glory…

Extract 3

STEVE: **Act Three: Redemption.**

ALEX: Lay it out.

STEVE: God pursues us—coming after His broken image-bearers to restore them. In this He is determined, relentless. He seeks to mend the communion that has been lost and to attend to the brokenness caused by our rebellion.

ALEX: How does he do that?

STEVE: He makes a start with an elderly, semi-nomadic shepherd by the name of Abraham.

ALEX: I've heard of him.

STEVE: Abraham is an honoured figure for Muslims, Jews and Christians—the narratives of each of these three religions reach back to him.

ALEX: So what does God want with Abraham?

STEVE: He wants to make him into a nation that will worship and walk with Him and turn out to be a great blessing to the rest of the world.

ALEX: So that nation is Israel, right?

STEVE: Right. Fast-forward 400 years and this nation is in slavery, captives in Egypt.

ALEX: Land of pharaohs and pyramids!

STEVE: Or for Israel, land of oppression and hardship.

ALEX: This must be where Moses comes in.

STEVE: Right again. God hears the cry of His enslaved people and is moved to rescue them, so He raises up a leader, Moses, to challenge the authority of the reigning Pharaoh and to lead His people out of Egypt to a land of their own.

ALEX: So comes the river of blood, the locusts, frogs, and all that.

STEVE: You know the story.

ALEX: I remember those vivid tales from a little bit of Sunday school. Scary stuff for an eight year old!

STEPHEN ELMES

STEVE: Well, the long and short of it is that Israel is delivered out of slavery and brought to a mountain where God gives His rescued people laws to live by.

ALEX: The Big Ten.

STEVE: Yes, and more besides—the Ten Commandments form the heart of a much fuller law code, held within a covenant (an agreement) between God and Israel. There is lots of detail, but the essence of it is a call to loyalty on the part of Israel to the God who rescued them, worked out in the practice of justice and mercy in every aspect of their living. This call comes from a God who declares His love and loyalty to His people, along with His purpose to bless the rest of the world through them. Remember, in the longer view, this is God's pursuit of us all—seeking to mend His broken-image bearers.

ALEX: I have at least a dozen questions buzzing in my head, but I'd like you to carry on for now.

STEVE: Okay. From the mountain, the nation is led through a desert land, to the land God has promised them—a rich and fertile land, 'flowing with milk and honey'.

ALEX: Would I be right in thinking that there were already people living in said land?

STEVE: Yes, indeed…

ALEX: (Interrupting) And that the next phase of the story involves the bloody conquest of those people.

STEVE: Right again…

81

ALEX: (Interrupting again) Enter the Warrior God! So where is the blessing for the rest of the world?...

Extract 4

Let's move on to the last big episode of the Jewish story... We find the Jewish people (Israel) in exile, in Babylon, the capital of the dominant world power of that time. Jerusalem has been destroyed, its Temple and city walls razed to the ground. The exiles are in mourning—brought to poignant expression in some of the songs we find in the book of Psalms.[6] Exile lasts seventy years. During this time, the prophets bring their disarming messages to the people, pulling no punches in presenting the unfaithfulness of God's chosen people and the judgement that has befallen them in consequence. Yet, the prophets say other things too. They speak of hope for the future: a return from exile and a time of rebuilding the nation. Some of these oracles reach further, into a future where all the nations of the earth will come to know the God of Israel, and the Creation will be healed of all its brokenness (hints at the fourth and final Act of the biblical drama). Now, amongst these prophecies of judgement and hope, another strand appears, intriguing and filled with hope. There is talk of one who will come to rescue God's people and restore righteousness and justice to the world. He is variously presented as a servant, a king, a saviour, and victor over evil—this is God's champion, pursuing God's broken image bearers, for that was always the plan.

ALEX: Okay, I think I know who this is: Jesus, right?

STEVE: Right. The Jews return to Jerusalem and begin to rebuild. Roll on four hundred years and listen for a baby crying in its mother's arms—born in a backwater of the Roman Empire. The Jews are under occupation. The long-awaited Saviour has just arrived.

ALEX: So you're about to tell me the Christmas story!

STEVE: No, I just wanted to step from the Old Testament to the New Testament and to make a link between the two. The point is that Jesus is understood by Christians to be the fulfilment of all the prophecies of hope in the Old Testament.

ALEX: Are we still in Act Three?

STEVE: Indeed—I told you it was the longest. God continues to pursue us. However, there is a step change—an understatement if ever there was one—in the coming of Jesus Christ. He is the long awaited saviour of the Jewish People—himself a Jew—yet, as it turns out, he has a much bigger job specification than anyone could have realised or imagined.

ALEX: Saviour of the world?

STEVE: Yes.

ALEX: So does the Saviour of the world command acts of violence against foreign peoples?

STEVE: You are like a dog with bone! But fair enough—no, he doesn't. In fact, he does quite the opposite. He teaches his disciples to love their enemies…

Extract 5

STEVE: The perspective of the New Testament is that Jesus' death reveals the love of God in way that nothing else quite matches. It is quite an extraordinary interpretation of events. A man who teaches his followers to love their enemies is arrested, given a sham trial and executed on a Roman cross. All manner of human brokenness comes into play: jealousy, cowardice, fear, political manoeuvring, crowd frenzy, and more besides. The result is that a good man—was any man more virtuous?—is hung on a cross to die. It is a travesty, a terrible evil, echoing so many other tragic, meaningless episodes in the human story. Yet—and this is the twist of all twists—in this hour of darkness, love is gloriously revealed. Jesus prays from the cross for the forgiveness of those who take his life. He loves those who have made themselves his enemies. He refuses to hate or retaliate in any way. Here is love, strong love, defined in flesh and blood.

ALEX: I get it. It's hard not to be impressed by Jesus in the way you portray him. But I don't see how this reveals God as loving.

STEVE: Let me explain. The New Testament writers speak of the crucifixion of Jesus as God's means of mending our brokenness and ending our estrangement—reconciling us to Himself and breaking down the walls between us. They claim that God is at work in the very hour when evil is doing its worst, when all seems lost, loving us back to life.

ALEX: I don't get it. How does a death do that?

STEVE: Well now you've raised one of weightiest theological questions of all time...

Extract 6

STEVE: [...] God enters our predicament and suffers the whole tangled mess of fallen humanity. He does not stand aloof, but enters in—vulnerable to the abusiveness and violence of His wayward creation. He bears it all and refuses to respond in kind—choosing instead to forgive. He absorbs our hostility. He takes away our sins. He does what is needed to mend our brokenness.

ALEX: I find what you have just said inspiring, but crazily far-fetched. I would love to believe it; I really would—for this kind of God, a Jesus kind of God, seems worth thinking about. But you're asking me believe in a man who is God!

STEVE: Wait until I tell you about how he rises from the dead…

Extract 7

STEVE: […] Jesus reveals who God is—more clearly and more vividly than ever before. This one who eats and drinks with sinners, prostitutes and tax collectors, upsetting the rule-bound religious, and teaching his disciples to love their enemies; this one who dies whilst forgiving his tormentors; this one who conquers death itself…

ALEX: *(Cutting in)* Okay, I see where this goes. Jesus shows us what God is really like. But doesn't that bring into question some of the earlier representations of God in the Old Testament? Isn't there a continuity problem? Or are we to understand that God had a personality change? Did he grow kinder and more compassionate with age and experience…?

Extract 8

ALEX: All right, I think I've pushed you hard enough for one morning. But you haven't finished the drama—by my reckoning we're still in Act Three.

STEVE: Yes, it is the longest, as I said. And you might say it continues still today. We really are still in Act Three! For after Christ come all the followers of Christ—living lives inspired and empowered by His Spirit. These include the first Christians whose stories are told in the pages of New Testament—who plant communities of Jesus-followers all across the Roman Empire—along with all who have followed Jesus since, in all the nations of the world and across the centuries.

ALEX: So the story rolls on. But what about Act Four?

STEVE: **Act Four** is the final denouement, when everything is brought to completion.

ALEX: The end of the world?

STEVE: The end of our rebellion and the re-making of all things. The Bible calls it the **New Creation**.

ALEX: So a happy ending?

STEVE: A glorious ending when God makes everything right—the culmination and fulfilment of every faithful act and every Christ-like action in God's world. All is brought to judgement, and everything is put right.

ALEX: Is this glorious ending foretold in the Bible?

STEVE: Yes, but spread throughout its pages. Here and there in the Old Testament we are given glimpses of the future God has promised—often through the writings of the prophets, who speak of a new order in which all warfare is over and the rule of peace is complete. In one place the peoples of the earth are depicted refashioning the weapons of warfare into agricultural tools.[7]

ALEX: So you believe this great transformation will come?

STEVE: More than that, I believe it is underway.

ALEX: Seems a lot to swallow... a far cry from the world I know...

CHAPTER 7

Framing the Same-Sex Discussion within the 'Big Story'

Various scholarly considerations of the handful of biblical texts that refer to same-sex behaviours have led to different conclusions on what is being referred to, and therefore what is being condemned. Traditionalist readings see a wider reference, taking in all erotic same-sex acts, including those held within loving, committed unions. Revisionist readings see a limited reference, taking in only unhealthy expressions of sexual desire: some abusive, some perverse, some wild and unrestrained, some integral to cultic worship. I have asserted the credibility of some arguments on both sides, and the entitlement of both traditionalists and revisionists to be in a conversation that is pursued with a high regard for Scripture. However, there is a limit to how far this discussion can travel while we remain in the limited field of the 'condemning texts'. We need, as Richard Hays puts it, 'to consider how Scripture frames the discussion more broadly'.[1]

At this point most scholars and pastors head for *the garden*— looking to the unspoilt Eden for a clear lead on the matter. The Creation narratives of the Bible depict humankind as made in the image of God, and the male-female union is central to this (Genesis 1:27–28 and Genesis 2:18–24) without any hint of an alternative (i.e. same-sex union). Karl Barth held that the male-female complementarity—including the anatomical complementarity of the sexual organs—is what it means to be made in the image of God.[2]

Not all would go this far, but most recognise that the ordinance of marriage is unmistakably cast in terms of heterosexual monogamy. Although, Steve Chalke has suggested that the second Creation narrative may present a norm without necessarily implying an ideal: rather like the norm of being right-handed, 'which never implies any failing of those who are born left-handed...'[3] The comparison does not hold up under consideration: for while left-handedness clearly falls within the creative intention implicit in our design, homosexual union does not. In fact, it evidently moves against it. Brownson has ventured a stronger argument, putting forward the concept of the 'kinship bond' in place of 'gender complementarity' as the key to understanding the one flesh union.[4] This is based on a careful study of the Scriptures, and is worthy of consideration, yet it still remains that that the Creation narratives present male-female union as God's design without any hint of an alternative pattern. Eden, it appears, cannot accommodate same-sex unions.

We are not, however, in Eden. We do not live in an unspoilt creation. In terms of the Big Story that unfolds in Scripture, we live in a fallen world that is being redeemed, moving towards the fullness of that redemption in the New Creation. While the original intentions of the unspoilt creation allow no alternative to marriage for the fulfilment of sexuality, the fallen-being-redeemed-world (where we live and move and do our ethics) holds the reality of same-sex desires for some, along with the perplexing moral dilemmas that accompany this reality. It will not suffice to point out that God never intended it. It is a present reality—one departure perhaps from the original plan among many. The pertinent question is what does redemption look like for those who are same-sex attracted? What does God do with this particular 'departure' (if that is what it is) as he works with loving ingenuity to redeem and renew all things?

I have just used a phrase that needs unpacking: *God's loving ingenuity*. We see it throughout Scripture. God works with our brokenness, even our rebellion, to bring about his redeeming purposes. Take the matter of kingship, for example. Israel calls for a king to rule over the people like the other nations (1 Samuel 12:12). God takes this as rebellion (1 Samuel 8:4–22), an affront to His kingship, yet He concedes and human kingship becomes a means by which God's own rule is mediated (Deuteronomy 17:14–20) and a pointer to the coming King whose 'kingdom will never end' (Luke 1:33).[5] We see God doing such things all the time. He takes our brokenness and waywardness and fashions something new. This New Creation in the making is not a return to Eden. Or to put it another way, God does not remedy brokenness by 'restoring factory settings'. The New Creation is new and is fashioned out of the disorder and brokenness.

I am aware that to speak of same-sex attraction as part of the brokenness of the world hardly seems positive and is very likely to cause offence. I recognise that this will simply be an unacceptable perspective to some, not to mention upsetting—striking at the heart of matters of identity and value—yet I believe it opens up possibilities that an appeal to the order of Creation does not. It allows us to ask what redemption looks like for those who are same-sex oriented—given that the New Creation does not simply restore what was lost in Eden. It allows us to consider the possibility that God might weave this *departure* from his original purpose into his ongoing creative activity.

Brownson is among those who have wondered at the possibility of an accommodation of those who live with same-sex desires within God's redemptive work. He points to Jesus' discourse with the Pharisees over divorce and re-marriage as an example of God working with the realities of the human condition—as Jesus states that Moses (and God by implication) only permitted divorce due to the 'hardness of heart' of his people.[6] The thought is that such accommodation might be suggestive of how God might work with those who live with same-sex desires. In addition, the way the church has held various viewpoints on the matters of divorce and re-marriage might be instructive: for it has had to hold in tension the high standard set by Jesus and the practical, pastoral reality of lives that need forgiveness and the possibility of a new beginning.[7] If those who re-marry commit adultery (Matthew. 19:9), and if this is understood as a sinful state that might be covered (redeemed) by God's grace, then perhaps those who live in faithful, same-sex relationships might be accorded the same opportunity to experience and grow in grace. Again, I fully realise this is sensitive territory— particularly in the inference of sinfulness with respect to same-sex unions.

What is helpful about such explorations is the appeal to the Big Story of Scripture, along with the great themes of the biblical story: including grace and forgiveness, redemption and restoration, justice and mercy. For while the Bible may be deemed to have nothing to say directly to those in loving, committed, same-sex unions (depending on your view of the condemning texts as already explored), there are strong themes and principles embedded in the Big Story that may give us what we need to address this and a whole host of other issues.

For Steve Chalke, the biblical principles of justice, reconciliation and inclusion, which he sees as the heart of Jesus' message and mission, are the guiding light. On this, Chalke is passionate, and it is clear that he writes from strong pastoral motivations, moved by the plight of those who have been marginalised and mistreated by the church, and determined to build a community that bestows acceptance on those who have found themselves *out in the cold*. He calls for the church to discover what 'real, Christ-like, inclusion' looks like.

In response, Steve Clifford, Director of the Evangelical Alliance of Great Britain, has declared that Chalke's concept of inclusion is not radical enough.[8] By this he means that Jesus' acceptance of those on the margins of society included a journey of discipleship and of transformation. Jesus did not condemn the woman caught in adultery, but he did instruct her to 'Go now and leave your life of sin' (John 8:11). Likewise, argues Clifford, to show love and acceptance to those of homosexual orientation without holding out the call to holiness, falls short of the inclusion characteristic of Jesus' ministry. Clifford's point is well made, though it does rest on the assumption that homosexual acts are intrinsically sinful and that holiness for the same-sex attracted can only be expressed in celibacy. What if God should choose to work in other ways?

Another attempt to work with key biblical themes and principles has been made by Richard Hays in his identification of three 'focal images': *community, cross* and *new creation.* [9] Hays regards these as finding a textual basis in all the books of the New Testament, highlighting the central and substantial ethical concerns of each text, and therefore suitable as guidelines for synthetic reflection. He makes use of them in considering a range of ethical issues, including homosexual unions. I would like to follow Hays' thread on the latter, while offering some other possible outcomes as we go.[10]

Employing the 'lens' of *community*, which holds the idea of being called to live as a counter-cultural community of discipleship, Hays reflects on how 'the biblical strictures against homosexual behaviour are concerned not just for the private morality of individuals but for the health and wholeness, and purity of the elect community.' Everything we do, argues Hays, affects the whole body of Christ and our witness to the wider society.[11] Turning to the lens of the *cross*, Hays considers the sacrificial love of Christ as the means of our salvation—a gift to all, for all have sinned—and as a model for our response to those who are of homosexual inclination, summoning not condemnation but sacrificial service. He also considers the call to die to self, as well as the transforming power of the cross (Romans 6:12–14), in their bearing on those who live with same-sex desires and seek to honour God in a celibate lifestyle.[12] Then through the lens of *new creation*, Hays considers what it means to live in the tension between the 'already' and 'not yet' of God's Kingdom (God's reign of justice and mercy).[13] So there is the present experience of God's grace for the homosexually oriented, knowing God's deep acceptance and forgiveness, and the power of the Spirit in the path of discipleship—yet for most, the battle with same-sex attraction continues. There is the 'groaning with creation' for the fullness of redemption (Romans 8:18–21). There is the hope of wholeness and completeness to come, taking our place in the New Creation. On this, Wesley Hill has written so movingly of the *accolade* that awaits the one who has struggled with same-sex desire and the call to holiness.[14]

Hays moves skilfully in employing his interpretative focal images (lenses) to arrive at a traditionalist position on same sex unions; yet it occurs to me that other outcomes are possible using his model. Starting with the lens of *community*, I would first comment that those who seek to live a celibate life will need to know the church at its best—no superficial fellowship will do, but only strong bonds of love, able to accept, hold, comfort and inspire. In addition, I wonder at the possibility of such bonds holding and helping those who decide to enter (or continue in) a same-sex partnership, having reached the conclusion that this is God's calling and gift to them. Such a situation would have implications not just for the couple, but also for the church and its surrounding community. It is very likely that some within the church would judge it to be wrong, while others shared and affirmed the sense of God's blessing on the couple in their commitment and love. The danger of strife and division in the church would be real. Yet, it might prove to be a growing point for the church: learning to live with difference, respecting the journeys of one another. It would be costly—in different ways to celibacy—but costly nonetheless (looking through the lens of the *cross*). There would be a level of social discomfort to work through. Perhaps there would be needed limits and disciplines— agreed with sensitivity and love—to the expression of sexual desire for those who are same-sex attracted. All of this is sensitive and contentious. Yet, I give this alternative use of Hay's model to show how a different perspective might emerge, in which God takes a loving, committed same sex union into his redemptive work as we (all) travel towards the future He has promised (*new creation*), where, incidentally, all our most intimate relationships will be transformed (Matthew 22: 23–32).

JOIN THE CONVERSATION…

1 What are your thoughts and feelings about what you have read? It may help you to write them down. If you are in a group context, take time to let each person share, listening carefully to one another.

2 I have asserted the entitlement of both traditionalists and revisionists to be in a conversation that is premised on a high view of Scripture. What is your reaction to this?

3 What are the big themes of the Bible that help us in respect of same-sex relationships?

4 What do you make of Brownson's notion of the 'kinship bond' (p. 88) as a key to understanding the one-flesh union of Genesis 1—2 (over and against 'gender complementarity')?

5 How do you respond to the idea of 'God's loving ingenuity' (p. 88)—redeeming and renewing all things in a broken Creation? Does it make credible the accommodation of same-sex relationships, even though these cannot be seen as part of the original intention of creation (as in viewpoint D)?

6 How might pastoral responses to those who are divorced and remarried help us think through our responses to those in same-sex relationships?

7 What do you think of my alternative use of Hay's 'focal images' (p. 92)?

CHAPTER 8

Group Conversation: Session Two

Church Youth Lounge: Friday, 21 March 2014—19:30 to 22:00

Present: Steve, James, Greta, Dru and Maureen

We opened with a short time of worship followed by an opportunity for everyone in the group to share any reflections since we last met.

Maureen kicked off by relating her recent encounters with two families, both of whom had a (grown up) child who had come out as gay. In one case the conversation had become somewhat awkward when Maureen had commented that it must be difficult for parents to cope with such a situation, a remark that obviously caused offence. Maureen said that she was somewhat amazed that these two encounters had occurred in the short time since she began her involvement with this group.

James had done some work on the Greek words in the texts that refer to same-sex erotic behaviours, which had reinforced his view that the texts had no real bearing on our response to loving, committed same-sex relationships. Greta had also been spending time with the same biblical texts, yet had come to the view that while some of them seemed to refer to particular expressions of homosexuality, others seemed to have a wider reference (i.e. condemning any sexual activity between people of the same sex). It was the first clear disagreement expressed within the group and was well handled by those present. However, Greta did go on to express a concern that she felt herself to be on the edge of the spectrum of viewpoints—given that there were none to represent viewpoint A—which felt a bit uncomfortable, and she even wondered if she was on her own as a 'B' in the group. Steve reassured Greta that views B to E were all well represented in the wider group, while acknowledging that the present sub-group meeting may have been somewhat skewed towards more 'accepting' positions.

Dru told us that she had been thinking about how important (or unimportant) her own particular views were: 'While I may not believe it is right for two people of the same sex to make a life together, what does it matter what I think?' This led us into a discussion about the different views that exist within our church community and the very small likelihood that we will all come to an agreement. *So how then do we craft a pastoral response?* We agreed that humility would be crucial and a commitment to the unity of the church vital.

Prompted by this, Steve told the group about a programme he had watched recently on a Premier Radio video broadcast, in which Rob Bell and Andrew Wilson, two well-known evangelical leaders with different positions on same-sex partnerships, were in dialogue.[1] At one point in the conversation, Rob Bell (holding an 'accepting' position) was asked by the interviewer, Justin Brierley, what was to be done about their disagreement on how to interpret the Scriptures regarding this issue. Bell replied:

Andrew is my brother: if we got out the bread and wine, we'd both take it. I understand that I read one way and he reads it another way. Is that it then? Do we just part ways? Or do you take the bread and wine, and Christ holds us together? Is there something that trumps whatever differences we have? [...] This is the bullshit that [...] pushes people away: when you have a particular conviction, all of a sudden your orthodoxy or your commitment to Jesus is called into question. [...] The tent might be a little bigger.[2]

Bell's response pinpointed a vital question for the group that we would find ourselves returning to often: is our position on same-sex relationships a fellowship-breaking issue—or is it possible that we might hold a range of viewpoints and yet maintain our unity and integrity as a local church?

In the second part of our morning, we took some time with two of the stories from the Baptist Union resource pack. The first story recounts the experience of a young man called Peter, who found the courage to talk with his pastor about his sexual attraction to men, and his fear that he would meet rejection if others knew about it. Peter desired to be baptised, but wondered if he would be acceptable. The group felt a lot of sympathy for Peter, were glad that he was able to approach his Pastor, and positive about his desire for Baptism—the group consensus being that same-sex orientation was not in itself a reason to forbid it. We felt that Peter needed a church community that would provide acceptance and support in working out his sexuality as a valued member of the church, and we aspired for our own church community to be a place where those who are discovering, and perhaps struggling with, same-sex desires could share this with others and be encouraged as disciples of Jesus Christ.

The second story we reflected on together involved a young mother called Tina, who attended an Alpha course[3] at her local church, and several weeks into the course made it known that she lived with her partner, Susie, and their little boy. The experience of Alpha brought Tina close to a commitment to Christ, and the Pastor of the church went to visit her and her partner. During the conversation, the couple spoke of Tina's newfound faith and their shared desire to strengthen their commitment as a couple through a civil partnership. They wondered if the church could offer them a blessing on their union, and also dedicate their son Jake?

For those holding views B to C, the case was extremely problematic—since it was far from clear how the traditional teaching on same-sex relationships should be acted upon here. Would Christian discipleship mean separation for Tina from her partner and the loss of a stable family home for Jake? Such an option seemed unthinkable. Might the challenge be made to Tina and Susie, in due course, to refrain from sexual intimacy? If so, how would that be ensured?

We reflected together on how those who encountered Jesus in the gospels rarely, if ever, had 'everything together' in their lives. In our experience also, people came to Christ with 'messy lives'. The good news of the gospel is that there is a welcome for all ('come as you are') and a path of discipleship for all, which involves transformation into the image of Christ. Yet, it is unclear for Tina what this looks like. Should she repent of her lesbian relationship and separate from her partner, or create appropriate distance within the relationship; or is it possible that the relationship could carry God's blessing and itself be transformed by God's redeeming grace?

Greta told the group that it was Tina's story—which she had first come across at the whole-day seminar held at our church in June 2012—that convinced her to volunteer for the working group: 'I feel a strong tension between wanting to encourage Tina's growing faith and desire to follow God and to welcome her, versus not wanting to condone behaviour that the Bible seems to forbid.' Others, in the group, felt this tension too.

A final thought that emerged from our discussions was the possibility that a church community might give Tina, Susie and Jake room to discover for themselves what discipleship involved, within a loving, supportive Christian environment holding a range of views.

AFTER THOUGHTS

Two members of the group sent me reflections on the session, from which the following extracts are taken.

Dru

'Thoughts have been germinating since a conversation last October with a lifetime friend who has been openly gay for the last 10 years.

He asked me what God thought of gay people and I replied that I believed he accepts them as they are but wouldn't want them to act on their same-sex attraction. This response was fuelled by reading 'Washed and Waiting' by gay Christian theologian, Wesley Hill, who has decided to lead a celibate lifestyle. I felt uncomfortable with this response at the time but couldn't pinpoint why.

'I have spent a lot of time trying to determine the biblical response to those acting on same-sex attraction and regularly step back and forth over the line between descriptions C and D. This is because in reality there isn't much to go on and I am now wondering if this is more about my human desire to know the "right" answer rather than walking humbly with God!

'I believe it is God's desire to heal and he is better placed than us to determine whether someone needs healing, what form this should take and when to work together on this project. Perhaps God is asking us, as his co-workers, to concentrate our efforts on creating an environment that encourages them to trust in him and his healing power. After all, there is plenty written in the Bible about what this might look like, and examples of where people have gone wrong in the past that we can learn from, knowing we shall often get it wrong too.

'Can church be a place where we are able to trust that the Holy Spirit will convict where change is needed? This may say more to the rest of the world about our faith than anything else. In his word God has made it clear how he wants us to be with each other as the Holy Spirit heals what he wants to heal, even when we cannot understand.

'Another Christian friend of mine who recently came out said to me that he did not know whether I thought his decision to lead a celibate lifestyle was right or wrong, even though I'd helped him through a very difficult time. I have a real sense of peace about this as it reveals I didn't get in the way of him and God. This is the opposite of how I feel things went with my other friend mentioned at the start—I think I need to invite him to dinner and explain things better.'

Maureen

'I found this session less engaging than Session One—I'm not sure why! I was disappointed Lewis hadn't responded and that Chris was unable to attend, so the group didn't have such a 'rounded' feel in age/gender.

'It was good to be able to be honest on views, but I was aware that my views were less thought out than others in our group who had researched passages in more detail than I had.

'I thought we each illustrated a different way of engaging in our discussion:

- James: an academic approach.
- Greta: a tentative approach, but very honest and deeply held views.
- Dru: providing helpful pastoral insights.'

CHAPTER 9

Is it Really Worth Breaking Up Over This?

Wild Goose: Thursday, 25 March—the time is 09:14

Steve and Alex are sat at their usual table.

CASS: Two Full English Breakfasts, the finest in town! Even if I say so myself!

STEVE: Thanks, Cass.

ALEX: Looks amazing.

CASS: I'll be back with your coffees.

STEVE: Thank you, that's great.

ALEX: So then, you were about to tell me about your second session with your group. How did it go? Did everyone show up?

STEVE: It was less than half the group, but I knew this would be the case. It was tricky finding a date everyone could make, so we arranged to meet in two subgroups for sessions two and three. I'll be meeting with the others next time.

ALEX: How was the dynamic with a smaller number?

STEVE: It was better, I would say. Although one of the group members was feeling that she was the only one in the room holding to a traditional view of the so called 'condemning texts', which, in retrospect was probably not the case, though it was how she perceived the situation. I did explain that the full group was well balanced across viewpoints B to E.

ALEX: Was that a difficult moment?

STEVE: Yes, but well handled by the group. It gave us the opportunity to re-visit our commitment to creating a safe and creative space for conversation—in which we value one another and the different views we hold.

ALEX: So did you get into those differences?

STEVE: Yes, though not in any depth. Enough to feel the distance between traditionalist and revisionist perspectives and to prompt what we felt to be a vital question.

ALEX: Go on.

STEVE: Well, its whether we allow our different views on same-sex relationships to become a reason for division in the church. I came across a broadcast in which a well-known Christian leader argued that this was not something over which we should separate from one another.

ALEX: What do you think?

STEVE: I think I agree. There are a whole range of issues over which Christians disagree and yet manage to keep fellowship with one another—including outlooks on women in leadership, divorce and remarriage, and so on.

ALEX: So is the issue of same-sex relationships of the same order as those, would you say?

STEVE: That is the question. Some would hold it to be more serious or weighty than the issues I just mentioned. Others would say we have made far too much of it—making it a kind of benchmark of orthodox belief. I imagine this is a question we will return to…

Cass comes to the table with two coffees.

CASS: Here you go. Don't let your food go cold—I worked hard on that!

STEVE: Too much talking, not enough eating!

Cass feigns indignation and returns to the counter. Alex and Steve dig into their breakfasts obediently, aware of Cass watching them. The conversation pauses for a few minutes.

ALEX: I'm thinking, surely it's possible!

STEVE: What?

ALEX: The church not having to split over this issue, or any other. Don't families have to do this all the time? In fact, any kind of community faces this challenge. Where there are people, there are potential tensions and disagreements—you just have to figure it out, surely.

STEVE: That is what we are trying to do.

Conversation pauses again for a moment or two.

ALEX: So tell me about the rest of your session.

STEVE: We spent a good amount of our time discussing two stories—fictional ones provided by the Baptist Union Working Group on Human Sexuality, though based on scenarios found in our churches. One was about a young man who found the courage to speak to his minister about his same-sex attraction; the other was about a lesbian couple that became involved with a church and began to ask questions about having their child dedicated and their relationship blessed.

ALEX: I am sure that stirred things up for you—the second one, I mean.

STEVE: It certainly did, although I have noticed that something a bit different happens when you start to talk about people—even fictional people—compared to discussing biblical texts. There something about a tangible, real situation that draws something different from us. Greta, who holds a more conservative position, told us that it was the story of the lesbian couple that really impacted her when she attended the whole day seminar I did with the church, and actually made her want to be involved in the working group. She felt challenged by it in a way that took her beyond arguments to responding to a unique human predicament.

ALEX: Yes, I can see that.

STEVE: It reminds me of something one of my lecturers at my theological college said to me years ago. It was something like, 'you can do all this study here and get your theology sorted out, then,

104

when you get into a church, you meet people, and everything changes.'

ALEX: I like that.

STEVE: I've never forgotten it.

ALEX: So what's next?

STEVE: I'm due to meet up with one of those 'real life' people this week for a coffee—a religious brother, who is gay, a good friend of mine. I sent him a questionnaire and he is bringing me his answers personally with the idea of us being able to get into a conversation.

ALEX: Sounds good—I hope it goes well.

CHAPTER 10

Brother Fidelis

Questionnaire Responses

Name: **Brother Fidelis**
Age: **47**
Current Church Involvement: **Religious Brother and Priest**

Please answer the following in whatever detail you would like to, typing your answers underneath the questions.

Tell your story

I was brought up in a Christian family with a rather conservative approach to human sexuality. I have an older male sibling. It was perfectly normal to attend church regularly and to be active in my Christian life in school (Christian Union/ Summer Camps etc). My Father had an Anglo-Catholic upbringing but lapsed; my mother had a Methodist upbringing but lapsed. On marrying they decided to go back to church and worship wherever they happened to be living. This meant I had a rather Conservative and mixed church upbringing in both Catholic and evangelical traditions (for which I am very grateful); these two traditions did shape my views of this and so many other subjects.

It is not easy to pinpoint when I realised my sexuality seemed different from my friends at school; but certainly by my mid-teens I realised that by inclination I was homosexual. I fell in love with a male friend while at College and this confirmed to me that I was gay.

This was very much at odds with my upbringing and understanding of the Christian faith. It led to years of unhappiness and seeking to "change". This involved prayer ministry, counselling and even the foolish notion that marrying might 'cure' me. By the time I ended my student days it seemed absolutely clear to me that this was not going to change and that this was to be my 'thorn in the flesh'.

I began to pray for the gift of celibacy, which God in His grace has given to me; I could not walk this journey alone so I sought to make an act of Consecrated Celibacy by joining a Religious Order who help me to walk this sometimes lonely path. I have found great fulfilment in all of my vocation and for me it is the only option for a Christian who finds that he/she is homosexual. I have received huge blessings from God in all this; where I so yearned for family myself, He has allowed me the joy of godchildren. I don't have *one* person with whom to share my life but I do have a family of brothers to walk this path with me.

It is not always easy... and the church as an institution is often where the pain comes from... but I still believe that the call to be a disciple has its cost and for me part of that was not having a life-partner with whom to share my life.

In what ways has your sexuality impacted your faith journey?

After years of real struggle with my sexual orientation, I still believe my faith is stronger because I learned that His grace was all-sufficient for me. I have never been angry with God; but I did pray for change that did not come and that was a hard lesson.

In what ways has your faith shaped your understanding of your sexuality and how it might or might not be expressed?

No doubting that my upbringing shaped my understanding of who I am; but I do not define myself simply by sexuality. I am a child of God who happens to be gay. And my understanding of that is that I am called to be celibate.

What other influences have helped to shape your understanding and convictions regarding your sexuality and its expression?

I suppose living a life of consecration since I was 23 has been a major influence as well as a support.

What is your view of those who have reached different conclusions to you about what it means for those of same-sex attraction to live as followers of Jesus?

I have no clear understanding of how, based on Scripture and Tradition, anyone can reach different conclusions. However, I listen with care and concern, but still worry that this can be part of a wider Liberal agenda that makes God fit in with the modern world.

To what extent have you shared awareness of your sexuality with family members, close friends, spiritual leaders and/or counsellors, and the church communities you have belonged to?

I have always been open about who (not what) I am; part of that picture is same-sex attraction. Family, friends et al are all aware, but I refuse to define myself by it.

What have been the most helpful responses you have received?

Most responses are reasonable; many don't really want to understand too much and I think that for family especially there was relief that I sought to live a consecrated life.

What have been the least helpful responses you have received?

Those, and now especially <u>in</u> the church, who try to say that things are different and that I should seek to find a life-partner!

How would you describe the environment of your current church (or the churches you have belonged to) for those with same-sex desires?

Hypocritical! Don't ask and don't tell! And from many even in authority a real lack of understanding of those who seek a life of consecrated celibacy.

What would you say to a local church that is seeking to respond well to seekers and followers of Christ who are living with same-sex desires?

Make the option of consecrated celibacy both real and honoured in the life of your church. Christ Himself was a celibate, after all. The 'cult' of the heterosexual family in the church can be alienating and unwelcoming. We are all called to be "Friend" by Jesus; not family…it is quite sobering to really look at Scripture and see really how the early Christians lived…socially, pastorally etc. If all we offer as a church is a model that some cannot share in (that is the 'family'), it is small wonder that those with same-sex attraction feel pushed… either out of the church completely or to seek for themselves such a life with those whom they are <u>by nature</u> attracted to sexually.

Join the Conversation…

1 What are your thoughts and feelings about what you have read? It may help you to write them down. If you are in a group context, take time to let each person share, listening carefully to one another.

2 Rob Bell argues passionately that our different views on same-sex relationships should not divide us (p. 93). How do you respond to this?

3 How did you react to the stories considered by the working group?

4 Take another look at Dru's reflections given after the session (pp. 98- 99). Are these helpful to you?

5 In conversation with Alex, I make a comment about how encountering 'real people' changes everything (pp. 104–105). Do you agree?

6 What struck you about Brother Fidelis' story?

7 Is being a monk the only realistic way for a Christian leader who is gay to find the support he needs? Is there a Baptist (or other denomination) possibility?

8 How do you respond to Brother Fidelis' appeal for our churches to 'make the option of consecrated celibacy both real and honoured…' (p. 106)?

9 How might churches better serve and support their young people with respect to discovering and expressing their sexualities?

CHAPTER 11

Group Conversation: Session Three

Church Youth Lounge: Saturday: 29 March 2014—09:00 to 13:00

Present: Steve, Erica, Monica, Richard, Patrick, Lewis, Abigail and Chris

The morning news took our attention at the start of the session: for at midnight it had become legal for gay marriages to be conducted in England and Wales, and the first gay marriages to take place in our Isles were reported all across the media. We sat together and watched some of the video footage capturing momentous events, experiencing a mix of emotions as a group: there was a shared sense of the joy in the occasions, and recognition of the usual wedding slips, such as one person not quite getting the name of their partner right, causing hilarity in the congregation. Yet, for some of us, this was mixed with a sense of unease and contradiction.

Following this, we had our group round up. For Monica and Erica, this was their first session, since both had been unable to attend the opening session. Monica talked about being 'conflicted'— growing up with a conservative teaching on homosexuality and then coming into contact with a lot of gay people in her work situation in America. She said that it was hard to 'hold all this together'. Erica talked about the journey she had made over many years with the issue, and how she had come to viewpoint E and was now comfortable with the idea of blessing those who chose to live in faithful same-sex relationships. Erica also raised the question of how helpful it is to categorise sexuality, especially for those in their teens, adding that once upon a time it was quite usual for a teenage girl to have a crush on a female teacher without this raising questions about sexuality. This got us talking about the relationship between sexuality and identity, and the view of Jennell Paris that we have mistakenly allowed sexual desire to define identity.[1]

FOCUS: ON DESIRE AND IDENTITY

Jennel Williams Paris has written stridently and perceptively about the way desire in our society has come to define identity—so that what we want is who we are. She reminds us that the terms 'heterosexual' and 'homosexual' are social constructs with a fairly short history, emerging in the late nineteenth century initially as medical terms.[2] The terms 'straight', 'gay', 'bisexual', 'lesbian', and so on, are more recent still. The question being posed by Paris and others is whether it is really so liberating to adopt such labels and categories; or do such definitions actually pigeon-hole or even diminish our personhood? We are (all) much more than our sexual desires. Paris has actually renounced the designation 'heterosexual' for herself, as a protest against desire determining identity.

Ed Shaw writes in a similar vein in his book, 'The Plausibility Problem', which explores a number of 'missteps' taken by the church regarding human sexuality, including a failure to challenge the popular assumption 'Your identity is your sexuality'—missteps which, according to Shaw, have rendered the Bible's teaching on homosexuality implausible. (Shaw experiences same-sex attraction and is committed to a traditionalist reading of the Bible and to celibacy.)[3]

The opposite extreme is of course possible, where sexuality is thought of only in terms of desire and its fulfilment. Eve Tushet argues to counter

If sexual desire can be easily tweezed away from nonsexual longing and love and adoration then yeah, sure, I guess I can see the point of calling homosexual desire 'disordered.' But that's not how *eros* actually works! My lesbianism is part of why I form the friendships I form. It's part of why I volunteer at a pregnancy centre. Not because I am attracted to the women I counsel, but because I wanted to find a way to express that connection through works of mercy. My lesbianism is part of why I love the authors I love. It's inextricable from who I am and how I live in the world. Therefore I can't help but think it's inextricable from my vocation.[4]

Tushet has a point. Our sexuality should not be regarded as a discreet component of our make-up, as if it is has no interplay with other aspects of being human. To say 'I am gay' or 'I am straight' refers to more than the direction of my sexual desires. Yet for some it may be saying too much, or too little. Ed Shaw muses on this

> If I say, 'I'm gay!', people think they know what I mean and don't ask me any more questions. But if I say, 'I experience same-sex attraction!' they're confused and so do ask me more. It allows me to communicate accurately what I want to say about my sexuality. I tend to think it's one of those areas of life where accuracy is quite important.[5]

Clearly a balance needs to be struck here, so that we neither de-value sexuality nor elevate it too high.

As for the basis of our identity, Paris offers our status as beloved creatures of God, and urges us to sit more loosely to social constructs that define us on the basis or our desires or anything else. In short, 'Identity comes from God, not from sexual feelings.'[6]

GROUP CONVERSATION CONTINUED

The rest of the group gave brief updates on their recent activities and reflections. Patrick told us that he was most interested in how we read the Bible on this matter. Chris said that he could not, at present see how the biblical texts could be read to move toward viewpoints D and E, though he was grateful to be in the conversation—for it seemed to him that 'God was in the conversation and that being about it was part of something bigger: the Kingdom of God coming and God renewing his creation.' Lewis told us how so many people in his workplace were asking him about the response of the church to gay marriage, and that this underlined the importance of doing what we were doing. Abigail said that she was 'coming from the other way, as a new Christian, wondering why we would not accept a gay couple but eager to learn from the group.' Richard shared how he could never imagine making a same-sex life-style choice as it was so far from his orientation, and reflected on how attitudes had changed in society and to some degree in the church.

Due to a lot of our time being spent on the group round up, we only had time to consider one of the stories in the Baptist Union Resource Pack, and we chose to look at Tina's story. There were similar responses to the subgroup that met a week before: a recognition of God at work in drawing Tina to himself, and joy felt in that; a desire to welcome and encourage Tina and her family in their faith; and a disquiet (for some in the group) with a life-style that was contrary to the traditional teachings of the church. There was agreement that the dedication of the child should be given, but mixed views on whether it would be right to bless the partnership formally in a church setting. It was felt by everyone in the group that the unity of the church could be severely tested by such an act, and that this was an issue in itself.

AFTER THOUGHTS

A number of the group sent Steve reflections following this session.

Monica

Monica wrote that she had found the session very engaging and had felt 'overcome by a sense of change, relief and peace.' She went on to describe how working through the (BU) resource pack had enabled her to reconcile two things she had previously felt irreconcilable.

'Before being part of this group, I have regarded the Christian view of homosexual orientation to be the only really embarrassing, shameful aspect of my Christian beliefs. This has been highlighted in the last five years as I have had many gay people in my life, and several close gay friends.

'While feeling ashamed of this aspect of faith and ashamed of the behaviour of churches I love, I've also felt a conflicting shame from an insecurity rooted in not feeling "spiritually enlightened" enough to have attained what my fellow Christians seem to portray so easily—a peace and acceptance of a black and white, anti-gay stance.

'I have found the opportunity to speak openly about homosexuality in a church setting deeply liberating, and sensed a shift in my perspective as a result.'

Patrick

'I found it helpful just to listen to others and get a feel for the different perspectives. As it was geared more towards stories than theology, it probably engaged my feelings more than my thoughts. I felt the group worked well together as there were differing opinions shared but all done in a sensitive and humble fashion.

"My priority has been to try and figure out where I stand Biblically and so that is where I will focus my efforts outside the group right now. I plan to do this through my own research and reading.

'My perspective hasn't changed as such but I didn't have strong convictions to begin with. As I read differing opinions and listen to others, I'm sure my perspective will be challenged.'

Erica

'As one of the older members of the group I realise that I have been thinking about this subject for rather too long! I recognised in others some of the thinking I have been through. I felt relieved that I could be honest without being judged as "off side" and that I could share some of my own reading. It was good to hear everyone's reasons for being there and particularly to hear from younger members how they wanted to know how to talk about this issue as a Christian with their non-Christian friends and colleagues.

'The most difficult aspects of all this are the pastoral situations and the need for wisdom and God's love when things are never as simple as they are in books.

'We have a choice as church to be increasingly side lined, irrelevant to how people live, and stick to the traditional views, or to believe that our task is to bring God's love to the gay community as much as any other, and that will not happen unless church stops making blanket condemnations of all gay relationships.'

CHAPTER 12

The First Gay Marriages and Some Honest Engagement

Wild Goose: Friday, 11 April—the time is 11:45

Steve and Alex have been chatting for an hour or so, talking about their families, their plans for the Easter holidays, and Alex's dislike of red tape (bureaucracy). Their conversation is just about to turn to Steve's research group.

ALEX: So you've had another session since we last spoke.

STEVE: Yes, it began rather differently with us watching media coverage of the first gay weddings to be conducted following the change in the law (midnight on the Friday before).

ALEX: Yes, I caught some of that—found it quite moving.

STEVE: We did too, though, as you might expect, there were mixed feelings in the group.

ALEX: My son, Daniel, showed me a YouTube video of the moments after the New Zealand Parliament voted in favour of gay marriage (about a year ago)—you should watch it, it's incredibly powerful.[1] After the announcement, the speaker is interrupted by a spontaneous burst of singing—a Maori love song. I have watched it several times and it always moves me to tears.

STEVE: Send me the link—I'll check it out.

ALEX: I will. So how did the group get on after viewing the morning news?

STEVE: Very well—I felt people were engaging honestly with one another and with the issue, and able to speak of the conflicts they felt within themselves. I was especially struck by the comments of the younger members of the group, who gave voice to the tension (or sense of contradiction) between what they had been taught in church about homosexuality and their relationships with gay friends. One of them wrote to me afterwards about her embarrassment over what the church teaches and stands for, and her sense of shame at being critical of the church that has nurtured her.

ALEX: Do you think this is a generational thing?

STEVE: Yes I do. It varies of course, but the young people I have spoken to are much less hung up about the issue and more inclined towards accepting views. It may be because they are more in touch with those who identify as gay. It's back to 'real people' again.

ALEX: So, do you have any more 'real people' to interview?

STEVE: Yes, a minister this time.

ALEX: Is he gay?

STEVE: No, he is leading a church that has received an informal request for membership by a man who is. I went to the church to lead a one-day seminar on same-sex relationships and how the church responds—to help them think it through. This is a follow up interview.

ALEX: I feel a bit annoyed about that.

STEVE: About what?

ALEX: Well, this poor guy applies for membership and everyone has to talk about it. It seems a bit unfair. I mean, how would you like the church to discuss your sexuality and lifestyle?

STEVE: I see what you mean. Though it's difficult to see a way round it—the church still needs to work out where it stands and what to do.

ALEX: Does it have to be the whole church community, for goodness sake?

STEVE: We certainly didn't speak of the man during the day I led— it was only the leaders who were aware of an impending application for membership.

ALEX: Well that is something.

STEVE: Although there probably came a point where the wider community had to make a response—in line with the Baptist way of making decisions.

ALEX: Oh yes, I remember that. Well I just hope that it was done with a bit of sensitivity to the person. I can't help feeling that it's somewhat exposing, and not very Christian.

STEVE: Well, I guess I'll find out more when I chat to the minister.

CHAPTER 13

Interview with a Baptist Minister

The interview took place over the phone on Thursday 24 April 2014 between 09:00 and 10:00, responding to some questions sent out in advance.

Q1 When did the seminar take place and where?

A seminar available to the whole church took place on 25 February 2012. The week before this there was a leadership 'taster' session (about an hour) and the BU materials were sent out ahead of this. The taster session was very helpful as the leadership were not all of one mind and the potential for 'fall out' felt considerable. Seeing the resources ahead of the leadership meeting and meeting you (Steve) gave confidence to everyone and allayed fears. The diversity of views within the group became apparent straight away and openness to honest discussion was engendered.

Q2 How many of your team or church community were involved in the day?

12 on Diaconate, most present.
20% of church community = around 50 or 60 people.

Q3 How would you say the day impacted you personally?

I found the day detailed and in depth enough to enable me to reassess my thinking and the various perspectives on this issue. I came away with a more rounded understanding—more 3D. Overall it was really helpful. It helped to sharpen my focus and to be more nuanced in my approach.

In the run up to the day there was some anxiety about the day among leaders. We were concerned to keep it 'in house' on this occasion, a little worried that some might come from outside to influence or disrupt the day in some way. As it turned out, the day went really well.

Q4 What would you consider to be the outcomes of the day for your team or church?

Overall, people found the day really helpful. One member of the leadership team said that they had shifted their position as a result of the day: specifically he/she had refused to go to a civil ceremony for a family member and now wondered if they should have gone…

There was quite a demand for the material following the day (people who had not been able to attend).

One person felt that not enough attention had been paid to the Romans 1 passage pertinent to the issue.

Q5 Has the conversation about homosexuality and local church response to those living with same-sex desires developed within your leadership meetings? If so, could you describe how and where you feel you have got to as a team on this matter?

Immediately, yes, but not since…
The culture of the leadership team (and the church) is accepting of diversity and respectful towards different views.

Q6 How (if at all) have the outcomes of the original day and subsequent conversations been communicated and worked through more widely in your church?

Apart from initial leadership reflections, there have not been further group conversations. There was one immediate pastoral decision to attend to (see below) and there are others that are likely to emerge, which we will take as they come.

Recently we put up a notice on our pastoral noticeboard signposting an organisation supporting those with same-sex desires (http://affirmingbaptists.org.uk/index.htm).

Q7 Has any kind of statement, policy, or teaching been constructed concerning homosexuality and the response of the local church? Please give details if so.

No—I would be wary of doing this. Something simple would not have the necessary nuances; whereas an attempt to be comprehensive would end up being far too complex to be helpful. We will take each situation as it comes.

Q8 What is your impression of the diversity of views within your church community on this issue?

The whole range of views is present, right across the board. The great thing is that this issue is no longer taboo—people can say what they think and recognise other points of view. There is not a desire to impose one's own agenda on other people.

Q9 How well do you think pastoral responses to those living with same-sex desires can be worked out in a community with a range of viewpoints on this issue?

A sense of being accepted has to be the starting point. From there, it is about working out what the right response is. It is not helpful for same-sex attraction to be perceived as an aberration (though we have to work through what Romans 1 is saying). Pastorally, we need to start from acceptance.

I would give weight to the journey the person with same-sex desires is making. If a person has come to conclusion that it is right before God for them to be in a same-sex relationship, then I would want to respect their understanding and for the church community to do the same. In the church I lead there is generous spirit that engenders this approach. I recognise that this is not something we do with other moral issues (e.g. adultery or theft), which highlights that there is something different about this issue (Christians have different positions on this).

Q10 Have there been any pastoral situations since the seminar that have required you to work out a practical response to those living with same-sex desires? Please describe what happened.

We had an application for membership from a man who is gay and open to entering a same-sex partnership (though not currently in one). We brought this to the church meeting following the day seminar on homosexuality, inviting discussion and holding off the decision to the next church meeting. At first the person in question was a little phased that his life should be so discussed when this did not generally happen when people applied for membership (why am I a special case?). I talked this through with him and stressed that he had made a long journey with this issue and that others needed time to process what was happening—which he was happy with. In the discussion, there were some who said they would leave if the decision was YES and others who said they would leave if the decision was NO. On the whole, there was overwhelming support for the man coming into membership, with a few quibbles around whether it would be appropriate for him to ever be in a leadership position or work with young people. We felt that to deny him membership when he was not actually in a relationship would constitute discrimination on the basis of his sexuality. Had he been in a relationship already this would have been a different matter and I do not think we would have had the fulsome support that was expressed in the final decision, which was to receive the man into membership.

Following the decision, one person kept away from church for a while, but has come back. Some people kept away from the church meeting that decided the matter also.

Over the years I have been aware of some in the church who are gay, some of whom have been in same-sex relationships. We currently have a couple that are in a civil partnership that have started coming to church. I am pleased that they have found a warm welcome in the church. One day this couple may seek membership of the church. If that happens, I will work this through carefully. It will no doubt involve a lot of heart searching. I find that my position oscillates on this matter. In the end, I would want to help the couple work out what is right and respect their conclusions. I would envisage the pastoral team being involved and at some point bringing a recommendation to the church meeting.

Q11 How do you see the way forward for your church in the matter of responding to those with same-sex desires seeking to follow Christ? You can indicate any challenges you see as part of this.

The church is generous in spirit and open to different viewpoints. This gives a good basis for working things out together. Alpha, a tool we use a lot, expresses this openness—giving room for people to find faith and work out what it means in practice.

We are coming to understand that people are not all 'sorted' when they come to Christ and that there is a process.

I desire the church to be a place where people find acceptance and room to grow into wholeness.

JOIN THE CONVERSATION...

1 What are your thoughts and feelings about what you have read? It may help you to write them down. If you are in a group context, take time to let each person share, listening carefully to one another.

2 Compare the viewpoints of Paris and Shaw with that of Eve Tushet on sexuality and identity (pp. 115–116). Are these positions incompatible?

3 How did you respond to the reflections of Monica, Erica and Patrick, sent after the session? Do you identify with any of their thoughts (pp. 118-119)?

4 What do you make of the observation that young people in the church seem more accepting of same-sex relationships than older people?

5 What struck you about the interview with the Baptist Minister?

6 How do you feel the church dealt with the gay man who applied for membership?

7 What do you think of the minister's decision not to set out a church policy on same-sex relationships?

8 How do you react to the words of the minister: 'I would give weight to the journey the person with same-sex desires is making. If a person has come to conclusion that it is right before God for them to be in a same-sex relationship, then I would want to respect their understanding and for the church community to do the same (p. 128).'?

A Message on Steve's Answering Machine from Alex

3 May 2014—19:00

Hey Steve, I'm really sorry, but I won't be able to meet up this month for coffee or breakfast—I'm having to work away a lot, so not as flexible as usual. I hope your last session went well, and the next goes well too—I look forward to catching up with you at the beginning of June. Don't work too hard. Cut yourself some slack!

Alex

CHAPTER 14

Group Conversation: Session Four

Church Youth Lounge: Saturday, 26 April 2014—09:00 to 13:00

Present: All except for Lewis and Monica

After worship and our usual group round up, we split into three subgroups to focus on three short papers—each group took a different paper and it was up to each member to decide which group to join. The first paper was an article entitled "'But the Bible says…?' A Catholic Reading of Romans 1' by James Alison, and was recommended to us by Erica who had been impressed by it. The second and third papers were write-ups of two interviews conducted by Steve, one with a religious Brother identifying as gay, and the other with a church leader who had hosted one of Steve's seminars in his church. We spent around an hour in our sub-groups before re-joining to report back.

After re-gathering, we took time to listen to each group in turn and to open up for questions at intervals. The resulting discussion was fluent and engaging.

ARTICLE ON ROMANS 1

James Alison argues that Paul's words about men being inflamed with lust for one another and women turning to what is unnatural are best understood as referring to the excesses of pagan temple worship.[1] In the small group discussion, James (group member) shared a little of what he had been discovering from his own research into the *same-sex passages*, including Romans 1, which concurred with Alison's conclusion that the root concern was idolatry and the destructive, unloving actions that arose from worshipping the creation rather than the Creator. Abigail found James' arguments helpful and felt that she was beginning to find an understanding of the biblical texts that undergirded her instinctive position (E).

Chris was less convinced of James' argument, yet told us that he was coming to terms with the Bible being unclear on this matter. He shared with the group that he was more at ease about this and that he felt there was a need to stay open to other views and maintain fellowship.

WIDER GROUP RESPONSE

Dru agreed that the biblical references to same-sex behaviour were not clear in their application to loving, same-sex unions.

Erica responded that in one sense it seems very clear in a straightforward reading, and in the way the church has taught us, which raises issues about how we read the Bible. There are other issues where this is critical today: like genocide—how do we read the book of Joshua today?

Steve observed that this is a key element in how and what we present to the church—we will need to offer something that helps people read the Bible well.

Chris observed that culturally we are more open to different perspectives coexisting today.

James observed that this is true in quantum physics, so that some quite counter intuitive understanding is allowing new possibilities.

Dru talked about the Bible as our authority, yet the nature of it not permitting easy categorical judgements (it is not clear on everything).

Erica brought in Luke 24 (the disciples of Jesus on the road to Emmaus) where we see the disciples reaching a new understanding of the Scriptures and Isaiah 56 where God includes people (eunuchs and foreigners) previously excluded. We see movement and development within scripture.

Greta commented that while it may not be clear what some scriptures mean, this does not mean we should therefore disregard them.

Erica picked up on the use of the word 'homosexual' insisting that it was a modern word inferring a disorder and so not appropriate to read into the biblical texts. We grappled a bit with this, agreeing on 'same-sex' (behaviour, relationships, etc.) as more helpful, but also that we did not want to be over-reactive if other words were used.

Steve commented (later) that the way we use words would also be an important aspect of our proposal to the church.

FOCUS: ON TRAJECTORIES IN SCRIPTURE

Erica talked about 'movement in Scripture' citing the acceptance of foreigners and eunuchs spoken of in Isaiah 56 as examples: where those who were previously not permitted to engage in temple worship are told they will find joy in God's house (56:4–8). This widening of the people of God, bringing in those previously excluded, is an important theme running through the Bible, and is best appreciated when the Bible is read dynamically and as an unfolding story.

One writer who has picked up on the dynamic nature of Scripture is William Webb. In his book 'Slaves, Women and Homosexuals' Webb sets out a systematic approach to biblical interpretation based on the idea of *redemptive-movement*.[2] Webb emphasises the importance of finding the underlying *spirit* of a text, which he argues is different from the *principle* underlying the text.[3] So, for example, while a principle-application approach to Paul's admonitions to slaves and masters in Ephesians 6:5–9 might yield helpful advice to employers and employees regarding their respective attitudes, a spirit of the text approach discerns how this passage combines with other references to slavery to form a *trajectory of liberation* that begins with the fairer treatment of slaves and moves towards recognition of the injustice of slavery.[4]

Steve Chalke appeals to the idea of a liberating trajectory in his argument for accepting gay unions, and makes reference to Webb's work.[5] Stephen Holmes has rightly pointed out that while Webb traces trajectories of liberation for slaves and for women, his hermeneutical method does not find one for those who are homosexual.[6] In fact, Webb concludes that the texts referring to homosexual behaviour all move in a restrictive direction compared to the original culture, and that no movement towards a softer or more accepting view can be discerned, nor any 'seedbed' texts to suggest a future liberation.[7]

It is difficult to deny Webb's conclusion. However, if, as some hold, the texts that refer to same-sex erotic behaviours have no application beyond the non-relational, exploitative forms well known in the ancient world, then it is simply the case that loving, same-sex relationships are not addressed by the Bible. There is no trajectory to assess. Though it may be possible to infer from other 'movements' in the Scriptures—such as the acceptance of those previously judged unacceptable—a liberating word for those about whom the Bible is silent.

Session Four Continued

Interview with a Religious Brother

Erica found the story very moving and felt such sadness that Brother Fidelis had felt so alone, and that the religious order was the only environment in which he might be nurtured and supported (what about those who are not called to ministry or to the religious life?). The priest did not see the church overall as nurturing or supportive of those who are gay. Erica also observed that young people in the church (whatever sexual orientation) are taught to be celibate (chaste), and for a much longer period than would have been the case in biblical times. She also observed the 'church splitting' potential of this whole issue and came back to the 'What kind of God?' question as the key question for her.

Chris and Steve found the issue of young people and celibacy really thought provoking. We went on to talk about how well (or not) the church supports and helps people in this position.

Steve made a reference to a website about Spiritual Friendship[8] which is exploring what a richer intimacy between singles (including between same-sex attracted people) might involve within the bounds of celibacy.

Dru said that sex is not the be all and end all.

We had a good discussion about the supportive environment needed by a gay priest, and what other ministers in other traditions, as well as Christians more generally, might need.

James made a comparison with the church response to Darwin's *The Origin of Species*, and said that his heart went out to him: 'If only church leaders could have got alongside him. Dear God, let us not do the same thing with homosexuality!' He added that we are in a much less black and white era (in science).

Greta commented that the church had been divided over Darwin's work—not all in opposition. 'In fact it is the media that has tended to emphasise the conflict—makes for a better story!'

Maureen reflected on how homosexuals were treated by the army during World War One.

Chris picked up again on the matter of intimacy and the need to explore it in church communities.

INTERVIEW WITH A CHURCH LEADER

Greta observed that the church was large and loving: 'a lot like us!' She picked up on the final comment of the minister about acceptance being key and how no one is 'sorted' when they come to faith, but on a journey towards wholeness. This still left a big question for Greta: what does wholeness mean for someone who is living with same-sex desires?

Patrick was struck by the fact that the minister had not reached a position on the issue and did not think a position statement would be helpful for the church, preferring to take it case by case. He felt this begged a lot of questions about how the church will negotiate the various situations that may arise without some agreed understanding and basic guidelines.

We touched on whether leaders should live by higher standards to others in the church community.

Richard made a comparison with the issue of women in leadership and the calling of Gill Hawkins (one of our ministers) to the Baptist Church in Bookham.

Steve observed that there were a number of important elements to this: (i) we were responding to a real situation, not an academic question (Gill's presence among us and her sense of calling), (ii) we had some help from one of the staff at a nearby theological college to work the issue through, and (iii) the church was prepared to make the call without having to resolve every issue. It seemed to Steve that these elements are there in the story of the church we were considering: a real-life situation (an application for church membership by a gay man); the calling in of some expertise to help the church (Steve on this occasion), and the decision being made without resolving all issues.

Chris put in that for him membership was about fellowship rather than having the same views.

Patrick asked a question: 'In the story of the woman caught in adultery, did Jesus condemn the adultery but not the woman?'

Erica asked whether we could really separate the sin from the sinner so neatly? She asked us to put ourselves in the place of someone who was attracted to the same-sex being told they were loved but could not have sex.

Others in the group felt this was not unreasonable if we believe that same-sex sex is sinful. Patrick felt that we could show love and acceptance without condoning wrong behaviour.

Maureen asked if we could really speak as Jesus speaks (who are we to make such judgements?).

Steve reflected on a helpful talk he had heard on the importance of *intention* when receiving people into membership. 'It is not about having our lives all sorted, but the intention to follow Christ and to let God bring us to holiness. However, this still leaves us with the question as to whether holiness for someone with same-sex desires is found in celibacy or in a loving union!'

Dru said that only God can change our hearts—all we can do is accept people for who they are and be there for someone while God works in them.

James made a comparison with smoking and how churches in different cultures held very different positions on this.

Chris made the point that with smoking there were no texts to grapple with (unlike the matter of same-sex unions).

James reminded us that for some in the church, the texts have nothing to do with loving same-sex partnerships (therefore, for some, the Bible is silent on the matter).

Erica made a different kind of comparison by reading from a book by James Alison (On Being Liked): an imaginary debate about whether left-handedness might find acceptance or be rejected as against nature/God. It is a humorous piece, but makes a good challenge.

Steve rounded off our morning by saying that a number of things were emerging for him that seemed relevant to the pastoral response we will be crafting for the church:

- The issue of how we read the Bible.

- The way we use words.

- The uncertainty about how to understand the texts referring to same-sex behaviours, and the fact of differing positions within our community (and indeed the wider evangelical community).

- The fact that orthodox teaching has over the centuries maintained a non-approving position.

FOCUS: ON BREAKING WITH TRADITION

Those who hold to the traditional teaching on the same-sex issue point out that the church has, from its earliest days, consistently understood the Scriptures to forbid same-sex erotic behavior, until recent challenges have been brought. Some urge caution on departing from tradition—insisting that this should not be done lightly. O'Donovan puts the needed caution well:

> No element formed by tradition can claim absolute allegiance. But the right to revise traditions is not everybody's right; it has to be won by learning their moral truths as deeply as they can be learned [...] The tradition may not have the final word, but it is certain they will never find the final word if they have failed to profit from the words the tradition offers.[9]

Over the centuries, of course, the church has shifted in its understanding on a variety of doctrines and moral issues—as illustrated by the Reformation and the Abolition movement. A living tradition is able to do this—responding to the questions and issues of our day to discern how the gospel speaks to us, and allowing itself to be reshaped accordingly. Scot McKnight has helpfully distinguished between 'reading through tradition' and 'reading with tradition'.[10] He holds that we should receive the wisdom of those who have gone before us, but not allow their decisions to be 'fossilized', since the tradition needs to find new and appropriate expression in our day. McKnight states that there are times when we will need to challenge the tradition—such as in the case of interpretations of Scripture that restrict ministry roles for women.[11] Some will of course see a similar need to challenge the tradition in respect of same-sex partnerships.

JOIN THE CONVERSATION…

1 What are your thoughts and feelings about what you have read? It may help you to write them down. If you are in a group context, take time to let each person share, listening carefully to one another.

2 Having read several exchanges between the members of the working group, who do you find yourself identifying with most closely? Whose ideas and concerns do you most easily relate to? Who are you most often disagreeing with?

3 How do you respond to Webb's view of Scripture as dynamic (p. 136)?

4 Webb concludes that there is no positive trajectory in the Bible in respect of homosexuals as there is for slaves and women (p. 136). Does this decide the matter?

5 As the salvation story of the Bible progresses we see a widening of who is included in the family of God, particularly in the New Testament. Could tracing this progression bring us to a more accepting view of same-sex relationships?

6 Is it ever acceptable to challenge long-standing traditions of the church? Where and when has this happened before? What might be the guidelines for such challenges?

CHAPTER 15

Group Conversation: Session Five

Church Youth Lounge: Saturday, 24 May 2014—09:00 to 12:00

Present: Steve, Greta, Dru, Richard, Lewis, James

We began in worship, with a reflection on the Hebrew word 'Shalom' (meaning peace and wellbeing as a gift of God), then moved to our usual group round up. Greta started us off by sharing some reflections on the previous session, including her feeling that our main progress seemed to be in 'recognising our differences and the difficulty of seeing a resolution ahead.' This observation resonated with everyone. One after another, group members began to speak of feeling somewhat heavy and demoralised at the seeming impossibility of finding a shared understanding that would serve the church in its discernment. Dru said that she saw the potential for upsetting everyone. Lewis shared that he had got really down about this recently, as it all seemed irresolvable. He had been thinking: 'It's great that we are doing this—but why are we bothering?' Lewis added that he couldn't face the session last time (partly due to 'other stuff going on') so had stayed away. Dru said that she also felt anxious about it all—especially with our unity as a church seeming to be at stake. Richard remarked that we can so easily get into our corners on this and many other issues, and that our expectation is often that the other person should change.

It was good for the group to get all this out on the table. Steve observed that the mood of the group had changed from the first session, where there was a certain excitement, even euphoria, at being able to meet and discuss an issue that was often avoided in churches. Now there was a shared frustration at the reality of diverging views that seemed unlikely to find resolution.

The expression of these feelings proved to be a turning point for the group, as we began to see the task before us more clearly. As James put it succinctly, 'we are all in agreement that we are not going to agree! So do we need to focus more on what to do with our differences?'

We began to consider how our church might fare at holding together different opinions on the issue of same-sex partnerships. Richard commented that we do this with other issues, such as with *women in leadership*, and reminded us again of the process we had worked through as a church before calling our first woman minister to serve at the church. Steve observed that the issue of same-sex partnerships may be more difficult than some other issues: 'If we disagree over something like how to read Genesis 1–3, this is unlikely to have practical implications; whereas, if we have a gay couple turn up at church...'

Steve suggested that given our different viewpoints (in the group and in the church) it might be that we set out a proposal that gives the 'benefit of the doubt' to those who feel called to a same-sex union. Greta wondered if we could explain to a gay couple coming into the church that there are different viewpoints within the church, encourage them to look at the texts and then, 'if they think it's OK, to come into membership.' James commented that the couple might not have the theological maturity to do this or may have already worked out their convictions. Steve noted that the key thing in Greta's suggestion was a conversation that acknowledged the range of views within the church—being honest with the couple and then supporting them to work out what to do. He also commented that such an approach would be challenging both to the couple and to the church.

Lewis told us that he could foresee some people leaving the church over this issue, and that this thought upset him. He recalled some difficult history in a church movement that he was once part of and how it had impacted him as a young person: 'It is important to handle "fall out" well. The world is watching the church—how we disagree and how we deal with fall out is vital...'

After a break, we re-gathered to consider a letter recently sent out to Baptist Leaders following a statement made at the Baptist Union Assembly earlier in the month.

LETTER TO BAPTIST MINISTERS

Received by email attachment in May 2014

Dear _____

During the year since our last Assembly we have encouraged conversations around our responses to sexuality and relationships—especially in the light of the Government introducing the Same Sex Marriage Bill 2013...

We've seen those conversations happen:
In churches...
In associations...
In colleges...
In gatherings of ministers...

Some have not welcomed the conversations because they say that you want us to converse because you want us to change our view...

Others have not welcomed them because they say that they have been talking for ages and nothing has changed...

It's important to remember that the focus of those conversations has been to try to understand and appreciate why others, who read the same Bible, think differently to me... or you... And to recognise where our shared values lie...

To recognise and appreciate all that is held in common and to celebrate our unity as brothers and sisters in Christ...

These are not issues that can be understood in sound bytes...

They are issues that on both sides are too often dealt with in terms of judgment and prejudice...

And they are issues that the media love to stir up and use against us…

I want us to rise above all that…

In terms of the 'new law' and the consequences for churches there are details on our website…

We know from 'the conversations' that there is a breadth of opinion in our union—There is a breadth of understanding and interpretation when we go to the resources of faith to consider issues of sexuality and faithful relationships…

But let's be confident that the absolute authority in all matters is the person of Christ—as he is revealed in scripture, interpreted in the community of the local church, through the power of the spirit…

I am pleased to say that all the conversations, that I have been involved in, have been conducted in very gracious ways…

So following the conversations and consideration at Council and through the Baptist Steering Group comes the following—to express where we are up to on the journey—which will serve as a backdrop to our continuing conversations and the way we will seek to behave….

This will be posted on-line on Monday—but they are:

- As a union of churches in covenant together we will respect the differences on this issue which both enrich us and potentially could divide us as we seek to live in fellowship under the direction of our Declaration of Principle 'That our Lord and Saviour Jesus Christ, God manifest in the flesh, is the sole and absolute authority in all matters pertaining to faith and practice, as revealed in the Holy Scriptures, and that each church has liberty, under the guidance of the Holy Spirit, to interpret and administer His Laws.'

- Upholding the liberty of a local church to determine its own mind on this matter, in accordance with our Declaration of Principle, we also recognise the freedom of a minister to respond to the wishes of their church meeting, where their conscience permits, without breach of disciplinary guidelines.

- We affirm the traditionally accepted Biblical understanding of Christian marriage, as a union between a man and a woman, as the continuing foundation of belief in our Baptist churches.

- A Baptist minister is required to live and work within the guidelines adopted by the Baptist Union of Great Britain regarding sexuality and the ministry that include 'a sexual relationship outside of Christian marriage (as defined between a man and a woman) is deemed conduct unbecoming for a minister'.

This is not intended as our last word—but it's something of where we are—and where we would like to be next... It is making a determined effort to keep the unity of our union, which is founded on the person of Christ...

It seeks to be true to our declaration of principle... and above all, our ecclesiology...

It seeks to reflect the overall direction of the Futures process that rightly acknowledges the local church meeting as the place of discernment as it seeks the mind of Christ in all things.

Please continue to talk...

Stephen Keyworth
Team Leader, Faith and Society

Session Five Continued: Reflecting on the BU Statement[1]

It was observed by the group that the statement is largely a re-affirmation of where the Union Council has positioned itself for some time regarding same-sex unions: affirming the liberty of the local church to determine its own mind on the issue, while respecting differences; affirming the traditional biblical teaching on marriage as foundational; and making it clear that for a minister to enter a sexual relationship outside of marriage is considered 'conduct unbecoming'. There is an important change, however, in the second point of the statement, where freedom is accorded to a minister to act according to the wishes of the church meeting, according to conscience, without it becoming a matter of discipline. Prior to this, the advice given by the Council to accredited ministers was that they should not participate formally in services of blessing, though they might attend such a blessing where it involved a close family relationship or friendship.

The statement stimulated a good discussion in the group and there was a high level of agreement among us. We all felt the emphasis on unity throughout the document was important and helpful, echoing our earlier discussion.

The changed clause (point two) was welcomed, as it seemed inconsistent to recognise the liberty of the local church to discern the mind of Christ (point one) and yet disallow a minister from following that discernment if conscience allowed.

The re-affirmation of the traditional biblical understanding of marriage, as between a man and a woman, seemed both helpful and important, even to those with more 'affirming' viewpoints. Steve asked the group if this clause closed the door on same-sex unions being recognised and affirmed in some way by the church. The group did not think so, feeling that it gave the right foundation for discussion.

It was the fourth clause that took the attention of the group for the longest part of our discussion. Was it fair that a church might recognise and bless a same-sex partnership, while a minister in such a relationship could be disciplined for 'conduct unbecoming'? While we felt the inconsistency, we came to the conclusion that the position was justified because of the likely consequences of such a relationship on the unity of the local church being greater than for a (lay) member of that church in the same situation. It was, it seemed to us, part of the call to lead: to be held to a stricter ethic for the sake of the wellbeing of the community.

In the last part of the morning we thought again about how we would present the outcomes of our work to the members of the church. The point was made and agreed that people would need time and space to work our proposals through: we have made a journey with this, and the church community will need to do the same—not hurried or pressured.

Reflecting back at the end, the group was feeling surprisingly positive about the morning—given the rather downbeat start. We were hopeful that a way forward could be found that respected our differences and expressed the unity of the church powerfully.

FOCUS: ON UNITY

Again and again the concern to look after the unity of the church has been voiced in our discussions. There is the clear recognition that the steps we take forward regarding same-sex relationships need to be taken carefully, recognising and respecting differences, setting the right pace, and seeking God's wisdom at every step. We are coming to terms with the unlikelihood of resolving our differences, and so have begun to focus our attention on how we might hold these differences in making a meaningful and loving response to those who live with same-sex desires. Yet as we set about crafting a paper to present to the church meeting, we are beginning to wonder how this will be received by a wider body of people, who have not had the same opportunity to explore and wrestle with the issues.

Beth Ann Gaede, in 'Congregations Talking about Homosexuality', reflects on the challenge of raising a difficult subject in church communities. She observes that many people in congregations become anxious about a lack of consensus on an issue and consequently 'some people do and say atrocious things when they are asked to reflect on difficult subjects.'[2]

This seems to be the case across denominations as well as within congregations. O'Donovan reflects on the experience of the Anglican church in the turbulent waters of the same-sex debate, and urges both liberals and conservatives to pursue the discussion with humility, patience and perseverance, and to regard the possibility of separation over the issue as the very last possible outcome.[3] O'Donovan is helpful in questioning both the tendency of conservatives to schism (distancing themselves from those outside their understanding) and the tendency of liberals to pursue a justice agenda that claims precedence over all other reasoning.[4]

In our own context, there are no synods to decide the matter for us, yet we would do well to heed the wisdom of O'Donovan as the conversation is opened up to our wider church community. The tendency to withdraw from those who we disagree with, and the urge to champion a cause, can both turn out to be ways of not listening well to one another.

Join the Conversation…

1 What are your thoughts and feelings about what you have read? It may help you to write them down. If you are in a group context, take time to let each person share, listening carefully to one another.

2 In session five, the group came to acknowledge the unlikelihood of resolving our differences. This initially put us in a low mood, but brought us to an important turning point. We began to see the potential of accepting our differences and working with them. Does this seem a good way forward to you? What is the alternative?

3 How do you respond to Greta's idea about giving 'the benefit of the doubt' to those who live with same-sex desires who may come among us—to explain the range of views held within the church and to give room for them to work things out (p. 146)?

4 Do you agree with the outcomes of the group's discussion regarding a higher ethic for leaders (p. 152)?

5 Is the unity of the church important above all else? Could this be overplayed?

6 O'Donovan characterises conservatives as tending to withdraw from those they disagree with, and liberals as pursuing a justice agenda over and against all other reasoning, and holds that both tendencies can easily alienate others (p. 153). How fair are these characterisations? Where do you see these tendencies evidenced in the debates about same-sex relationships and other issues?

CHAPTER 16

It Hadn't Really Sunk In…

Wild Goose: Friday 6th June—the time is 10:15

Steve and Alex have just got their coffees and some generous slices of cake.

ALEX: I feel I've got a lot to catch up on.

STEVE: Yes, it's been eventful.

ALEX: Give me the highlights.

Steve talks to Alex about the sessions in April and May for an hour or so. Alex is especially interested in how the group ended in the May session.

ALEX: So there was a bit of turn around?

STEVE: Absolutely, the group started off in the doldrums and ended up bright and hopeful. It was the realisation and acceptance that we were not going to be able to resolve our differences that actually moved us on—to thinking about how we might hold those differences lovingly and creatively.

ALEX: Hadn't you realised that before?

STEVE: Sure, I think we had an idea of it early on, but it hadn't really sunk in for the group until this session.

ALEX: So what are you going to do with that?

STEVE: We're going to keep talking.

ALEX: And where will that take you?

STEVE: I'm not really sure.

ALEX: Steve, do you ever get nervous or worried about all this?

STEVE: To be honest, yes. I worry sometimes about not arriving anywhere. It would seem very weak just to report to the church that we hold a range of views and that we saw no likelihood of resolving our differences!

ALEX: What about the creative way forward?

STEVE: Yes, I believe we'll find our way. It's just in my less optimistic moments…

ALEX: I understand.

STEVE: My other worry—now that you've got me started down this track—is finding a way forward that the group are agreed upon and then meeting resistance in the church or causing upset. I imagine people writing me letters or resigning their membership.

ALEX: I guess you'll have to take what comes—all part of the process.

STEVE: I guess.

There is a short pause in the conversation.

ALEX: How is your friend, the monk?

STEVE: Very well—I met up with him a few weeks ago and he introduced me to a friend of his, a minister in an ecumenical project.

ALEX: What's one of those?

STEVE: Oh, it's where two or more Christian traditions have been brought together in one church. So it might be a combination of Baptist and Anglican for example.

ALEX: So, what is his situation—the minister I mean?

STEVE: Really interesting. He has been grappling with the issue of same-sex partnerships for years, and has travelled from a conservative position to an accepting, supportive stance. There is a gay couple in the church. They have been welcomed well and are much loved—part of the church family. Yet the church holds a range of views on same-sex unions, so is trying to work out, in conversation with the couple, how best to encourage them and to keep integrity. Wesley, the minister, told me that he was due to meet with his ECC (Ecumenical Church Council) to consider the matter of membership.

ALEX: How about you try to meet the couple? It would be good to get their story?

STEVE: It's already arranged. I'm going to join them for tea and cake. Wesley will be there too.

ALEX: I would love to hear how you get on.

STEVE: We can meet soon after if you like. Do you have your diary?

CHAPTER 17

Simon and Jim

An informal interview conducted by Steve Elmes with Simon and Jim, and their pastor, Wesley—12 June 2014. The style of the interview was to encourage a free-flowing story. My prompting questions are not included.

SIMON: My Dad was a vicar (now retired); my sister and my aunt are vicars, and my mum is a reader in the church of England—so I was born into the church!

By the age of 12 I knew I was different. By the age of 16 I knew for sure I was gay, but I 'buried it'. I believe now I was made this way...

I remember hearing Dad preaching against homosexual lifestyles—it was black and white, the homosexual lifestyle was wrong and led to damnation; a choice could be made to change—no discussion.

I found it hard to build friendships (with either sex) because part of me was hidden and denied.

At Reading University (age 18–21) I threw myself into the Christian Union (CU)—it was a way of absorbing myself, and my energy. Two or three girls from the CU made advances, which I had to fend off in order to be truthful to them. I was on the CU committee, looking after international students—I loved this, and did it passionately.

Later I joined 'Friends International' for a year at Surrey University and at the same time attended X Church in Y. The church adopted and salaried me to work with International Students.

During my time at X Church, the Senior Minister made his views on gay issues very clear. It was at the time when a well known Christian leader at the time 'came out'. After my minister had heard the news he told me that he was so disgusted he had got out and vomited down the side of his car!

I prayed to be straight often—but it didn't happen; this brought frustration and anger. My brother was (and is) a *Jack the lad*, a stereotypical man.

At age 24 I moved to Brighton where I found a new job working for a language school at Sussex University. Being Brighton I was suddenly enveloped in this 'cocoon of acceptance' of the whole gay thing…

I Joined an Anglican church. After four or five months I had an emotional moment—I realised I had to find out, 'is this me?' I went on the Internet to a chat room and started talking to another gay man. We had long conversations for around three weeks. Then he came to visit me. He offered a 'pretend date', to see how it felt for me. We spent the day together: we sat on a bench and talked, walked on the pier, held hands, had dinner… I felt a sudden release within me, it felt so right…

I wrote to my church to tell them I would not be coming anymore— I could not see the two things (my faith and my sexuality) holding together…

For six months this sense of release overwhelmed everything…

After a year I met Jim in a nightclub. I found him very attractive but it took me a while to get him to notice me…

JIM: I was drunk, arrogant and horrible—Simon came on to me but I didn't treat him well. However, we did fix a date for the following evening.

Simon was living a double life—none of his family knew, nor most of his friends.

SIMON: I discovered by accident that my best friend was gay! I spotted him at a gay club! So I called him and told him I had seen him. So we met for coffee. We 'outed' each other…

JIM: I was 8 when my father died. He was in the army so our family was abroad all the time. After his death, Mum sent me to a boarding school for sons of military personnel. By age 12 I knew I was attracted to the same sex. The thing was, school was homophobic. In the dorms there were posters of White Snake and Def Leopard. I had Abba posters by my bed and Charlie's Angels! I stood out, there was obviously something different about me!

I was a church prefect and religion was important to me—mum was a non-practicing catholic. I hated gays: I could not really acknowledge my sexuality to myself or others—I would have been beaten up.

I had girlfriends, and at college I got engaged—but the time came when I had to admit I could not carry on to my fiancé. She said she knew all along. I asked why she had not broken off the relationship. She said she loved me.

The matron at school noticed my sensitivity. I was the only person who did not have a dad and I got bullied…

At college I worked out that I liked women too—the whole 'bi-sexual' thing began to make sense.

I moved to Edinburgh and just lost myself in work. My best friend disowned me. He asked if I ever fancied him. I said, 'Don't flatter yourself!'

I joined the airline industry (the gay lifestyle is a 'given' there) where I could just be me.

At 24 I met Gabrielle, a Swiss-German catholic man, whose parents disagreed strongly with the relationship. He died of cancer in 1996. I was left feeling quite desperate. Everyone I had loved had gone. I tried to commit suicide five years after Gabrielle had died.

It was through meeting Simon that things changed and I began to rediscover my faith.

JIM & SIMON: We have been together for ten years, both working for Virgin Atlantic as on board managers. Virgin have been fantastic: really supportive, allowing us to have compatible rotas, really good about time off for medical reasons (Simon was found to have the same cancer that Gabrielle died from).

JIM: There came a point when I challenged Simon about his double life. We had been together two years. I said I did not want to be Simon's 'dirty secret' any longer. So Simon agreed to tell his brother, sister and parents.

SIMON: I told my sister first, in a hotel (she was not a vicar at this point but a youth worker). She wasn't too surprised; though she had no idea I had been with Jim for two years!

I told my brother over the phone—his wife had told him after the second time she had met me that I was gay! However, my brother had never really believed it. When others asked about my lack of girlfriends, he would just say I was shy.

I wrote a letter to my parents and asked them not to respond until twenty-four hours had passed. My mum called me and was in floods of tears. She told me that they were shocked but would always love me. My Dad was in denial at first, saying it was a phase. He came to terms with it and has allowed it to take him on a journey—revisiting his theology, for which he has thanked us.

In the December following the October I 'came out' to my parents, they sent a Christmas letter out to around 600 people sharing the news! There were just two negative responses among them.

JIM: I told my mum over the phone. I had been speaking of Simon as my Landlord and she said, 'He's not your Landlord, he's your lover!' We talked and she said, 'I love you more now than I did five minutes ago, I am only sad that I was not there for you when you were so sad and alone with this.'

Through Simon I found my faith again—I am allowed to love God and God loves me and sent Simon to me. I gained a mum and dad. It turned out that they were not the monsters I imagined them to be!

The churchwarden at Simon's Dad's church warned him: if you don't report your son I will report you to the Bishop (who was gay by the way)—he (the Warden) later left the church.

A few months after we had met, I told Simon I loved him. He said that was nice and that he would tell me when he felt the same. We go through the same things that straight couples go through. On the third time of asking, Simon said 'yes', but got cold feet when getting the suits fitted.

SIMON: My brother helped me—he told me that it was the best thing that had happened to me and to 'sort it out'! He says that my relationship with him improved so much after he learned that I was gay.

JIM: Our one thing in common is our love and trust for God.

We were joined by civil partnership…

No religion is allowed at civil ceremonies—not even religious based music like Handel's Messiah. So we sneaked a little religion in: our rings were engraved with words from Song of Solomon: 'I am my beloved's and he is mine' (6:3).

SIMON & JIM: After the ceremony, the registrar left the room. She said she regretted this but was required to. Simon's Dad went forward to give a blessing in front of everyone. There were around sixty-five people, around 60% gay and 40% straight. It was a massive witness to all our gay friends! Simon's Dad was inundated by our gay friends wanting to know more about the journey he had made with this and what he thought.

It was five years ago that we entered a civil partnership. It has been five years since Simon's chemo. treatment, since which he has been in remission.

We moved to Camberley in 2009. When we came, we wrote to five churches—we were honest, declaring ourselves to be committed Christians and a gay couple. Two responded—one said he personally did not have a problem with this, but that he imagined some in the congregation would, and advised us to look elsewhere. The other said: 'why wouldn't you be welcome? We already have a lesbian couple in the congregation.' We went to this church and joined a house group.

This was good for a time. Then the Vicar retired and our house group dissolved and we found ourselves feeling a bit lost. It was an aging congregation and we had never really built strong relationships, though all accepted us.

Then Wesley sought us out. Simon had known him before at the church where he had been a curate, and there was a family connection too.

(Wesley is the Priest/Minister at an ecumenical project.)

WESLEY: I had been on a journey with this for a long time: I was raised with a conservative view, but came to question it—nearly lost my faith over it. I have come to believe that the scriptures referring to homosexuality are not talking about the kind of relationship that Simon and Jim have. They are talking about something else. I know there is the wider biblical witness to consider and would love to be able to talk more with you about this (directed at the interviewer, Steve).

We have brought the matter of Simon and Jim coming into membership to the ECC (Ecumenical Church Council—our leadership team). The council of twelve discussed this at length and came to the recommendation that we should bring Simon and Jim into membership (eight in favour, four against/not sure, with the four willing to go with the outcome).

The church has been brilliant in welcoming and loving Simon and Jim, though it is clear that not all can square this with their understanding of Scripture.

A letter has been sent out to members to take things forward…

Join the Conversation…

1 What are your thoughts and feelings about what you have read? It may help you to write them down. If you are in a group context, take time to let each person share, listening carefully to one another.

2 What are your reactions to Simon and Jim and their stories? What stands out for you? What thoughts and/or questions are provoked in you?

3 What factors were at play in the losing and re-discovery of faith for Simon and Jim?

4 How do you react to the way the various churches in their stories responded to them?

5 What might be learned from Simon and Jim's experiences about how a church community might welcome and support a gay couple?

CHAPTER 18

Where From Here?

Wild Goose: Friday, 13 June—the time is 14:00

Steve and Alex have just sat down. Coffees are ordered and on their way.

ALEX: How are you, my friend?

STEVE: Just a little weary if I'm honest.

ALEX: Not surprising. You seem to go at quite a pace—fit a lot in.

STEVE: Sure, but I try to take breaks and find some calm when I can. I'm pretty good about keeping to my day-off.

ALEX: That's every Tuesday, right? How do you spend the time?

STEVE: I usually try to get out for a walk on the common. We're incredibly blessed to have it right on our doorstep.

Cass arrives with two coffees. Alex and Steve chat for some time, talking about leisure time and films they have recently watched.

ALEX: So then, tell me about your encounter with the couple you mentioned. How did it go?

STEVE: Really well. I liked them both very much and found their stories fascinating.

ALEX: Just fascinating?

STEVE: Not just fascinating—moving, really moving. I was quite undone, to be really honest.

ALEX: That's more like it.

STEVE: Both of them told of how they had lost their faith at the time when they were coming to terms with their sexuality, seeing no compatibility between being 'gay' and living as a follower of Christ. The loss (of faith) felt deeply sad, and yet there was a sense of liberation too—no longer having to hide or live a lie. Both rediscovered their faith later on, and that impacted me too—especially hearing about how their family members responded so well. I was especially struck by Simon's brother saying how his relationship with Simon had been so much better after he had 'come out'…

Steve continues to share his experience of meeting Simon and Jim. After about twenty minutes, Cass interrupts.

CASS: Hey guys, I need to let you know we are closing up in about fifteen minutes.

STEVE: No problem—we'll be moving along soon.

Alex and Steve both finish their coffees.

ALEX: So, let's use the time we have well. I want to know where you've got to with all of this. Are you reaching any conclusions—even tentative ones?

STEVE: Let me see what I can gather up. I guess the first thing is that there are different viewpoints within the church on same-sex relationships that are very unlikely to be resolved. This is despite a shared commitment to the Bible as God's inspired and authoritative Word to us. Not that this is the only issue over which Christians differ—coming to the same Scriptures with due respect and submission, and coming to different conclusions. Yet we seem to be able to hold other differences with less discord and more grace.

ALEX: Do you think that the church can find its way to holding difference well in respect of same-sex unions?

STEVE: I hope so, for I genuinely believe that both traditionalists and revisionists are entitled to be in the conversation we are having—that there are credible arguments on both sides.

ALEX: Some would take issue with that claim, I think.

STEVE: I am sure you're right, but I think there is a need for humility, recognising the possibility that we might not always be right. None of us have the complete picture. I have appreciated one member of the group who has kept saying that he does not think the Bible is clear on same-sex relationships, but that he is content to live with the uncertainty and stay in the conversation. I find that really helpful. Even when we are much more certain of what we think, we need to take care not to become arrogant or seek to disenfranchise those who disagree with us. I am reminded, as I speak, of a verse in the Bible that describes our life on earth as like looking at a dim reflection in a mirror, awaiting a time to come when we will see clearly (1 Corinthians 13: 12). We simply don't have full knowledge— none of us. Recognising this will certainly help us work with our differences.

ALEX: So how does this go forward for you?

STEVE: Well, I think it is what you say: we need to find a way of holding our differences well, creatively—as opposed to destructively or divisively. Recognising the creative potential of keeping our unity in the face of difference is the key. I feel that a great blessing can be unleashed if we can work this out—that a community that holds its differences well will forward the mission of Christ much more effectively than one that either ignores them or falls out over them.

ALEX: What does all that mean to your celibate monk and your gay couple? I love the high sounding rhetoric of unity in diversity, but when the rubber hits the road…

STEVE: Good challenge, yes, what I have said needs to be translated into action. That is why we need to keep at it—the group I mean. Engaging with the stories of real people, for whom this is not just a discussion topic, will be crucial. People like Jonathan, Brother Fidelis, Simon and Jim.

ALEX: Do you think it is possible that your church might provide a loving, caring environment for both the celibate and the gay couple?

STEVE: It's a challenging thought—but I certainly want to work out what following Jesus might mean for each of them and be part of that.

ALEX: Okay, enough for now—nearly time to go.

All the other customers have left the café, leaving only Steve and Alex with Cass, who is wiping down tables. Steve and Alex begin to put on their jackets when Cass suddenly pulls up a chair to join them.

CASS: (*Nervously*) I've been hearing a bit of your conversation—a bit hard not to if I'm honest…

STEVE: Sorry Cass.

CASS: No, it's okay—I like my customers to feel at home and able to talk about whatever they want to. I love the buzz. It's just that…

Cass's voice trails off and she looks around her before fixing her gaze on Steve.

CASS: Well I've heard you talk about sex a lot, or sexuality I should say, and… well… I know you're a vicar, or minister or something… and… I'm sorry I'm not making any sense. The thing is…

TO BE CONTINUED

ABOUT THE AUTHOR

Stephen Elmes lives in the town of Bookham with his family. He is the Lead Minister of Bookham Baptist Church, a church with a big heart and a vision to grow fruitful followers of Jesus who make a difference wherever they are. Steve's gifts are in teaching, storytelling, and helping people to grow in their faith and work out their calling. Over the past eight years, he has been helping churches in the South East of England to have a conversation about same-sex relationships. This is Steve's first book.

If you would like to give any feedback on this book, email steveelmes.wildgoose@gmail.com

NOTES

Chapter 2: Coming to An Arrangement

[1] An erotic relationship between a man and a boy, socially accepted within Greek and Roman Societies.

Chapter 3: So You Call This Research?

[1] See John W. Cresswell, *Research Design: Qualitative, Quantative, and Mixed Method Approaches,* 2nd edn (Thousand Oaks, CA, Sage Publications, 2003) pp. 1–26 for a good comparison of research approaches.

[2] Hans G. Gadamer, *Truth and Method*, (London: Sheed & Ward, 1981), p. 358.

[3] The story of the English Baptists pioneers is well told in detail by Ian M. Randall in *Communities of Conviction: Baptist Beginnings in Europe* (Schwarzenfield, Germany: Neufeld Verlag, 2009) pp. 13–48.

[4] Nancy E. Bedford, 'Little Moves Against Destructiveness: Theology and the Practice of Discernment' in *Practicing Theology: Beliefs and Practices in Christian Life*, ed. by Miroslav Volf and Dorothy C. Bass (Grand Rapids: Eerdmanns, 2002), 157–181 (p. 158).

[5] Helen Cameron, et al., *Talking about God in Practice: Theological Action Research and Practical Theology*, (London: SCM, 2010), p. 36.

[6] Baptist Union, *Declaration of Principle* http://www.baptist.org.uk/Groups/220595/Declaration_of_Principle.aspx

Chapter 4: First Gathering (Session One)

[1] Baptist Union Human Sexuality Working Group, *Baptists Exploring Issues of Homosexuality: How Baptists Might Think Biblically and Theologically about Homosexuality*. Papers for the Educational Process, extended and formatted for use by Stephen Elmes for the facilitation of conversations in churches.

[2] Baptist Union, *Declaration of Principle* http://www.baptist.org.uk/Groups/220595/Declaration_of_Principle.aspx

[3] See Chapter 7—Framing the Same Sex Discussion…

[4] For a good overview see Carl S. Keener and Douglas E. Swartzendruber, 'The Biological Basis of Homosexuality' in *To Continue the Dialogue: Biblical Interpretation and Homosexuality*, ed. by C. Normal Krause, Living Issues Series, I (Ontario: Pandora Press,

2001), 148–173 (pp.151–164).

[5] Keener and Swartzendruber, p. 165.

[6] Stanton L. Jones and Mark A. Yarhouse, *Homosexuality: The Use of Scientific Research in the Church's Moral Debate* (Illinois, InterVarsity Press, 2000), pp. 47–91.

[7] Jones and Yarhouse, pp. 54–58.

[8] Carl Keener and Douglas E. Swartzentruber, p. 150.

[9] Jones and Yarhouse, pp. 81–83.

[10] Jones and Yarhouse, pp. 83–84.

[11] Lawrence S. Mayer and Paul R. McHugh, Sexuality and Gender: Findings from the Biological, Psychological, and Social Services in *The New Atlantis: A Journal of Technology and Society* (No. 50—Fall 2016), p. 7.

[12] Mayer and McHugh, p. 7.

[13] Leanne Payne, *The Broken Image: Restoring Sexual Wholeness Through Healing Prayer*, 1st British edition (Eastbourne: Kingsway Publications Ltd, 1989), p. 36.

[14] Payne, pp. 42–46.

[15] Jeremy Marks, *Exchanging the Truth of God for a Lie: One man's spiritual journey to find the truth about homosexuality and same–sex partnerships*, second edn (Surrey: Courage UK, 2009), p. 6.

[16] Marks, pp. 55–58.

[17] Jones and Yarhouse, p. 133.

[18] Jones and Yarhouse, p. 148.

[19] Baptist Union Human Sexuality Working Group, Section entitled 'Sexual Diversity', Table: *Reported homosexual and heterosexual attraction and experience*. More recent and extensive data can be obtained from The Lancet (free registration required), *Sexual Behaviour in Britain: Partnerships, Practices and HIV risk behaviours*, by Anne M. Johnson and others, Table 4, http://www.thelancet.com/journals/lancet/article/PIIS0140–6736(01)06883–0/fulltext#back–bib1 and on the Natsal (National Survey of Sexual Attitudes and Lifestyle) website, which provides comparison of surveys in 1990 (Natsal–1) 2000 (Natsal–2) and 2010 (Natsal–3), http://www.natsal.ac.uk/home.aspx.

[20] Mona Chalabi, *Gay Britain: what do the statistics say?* (The Guardian, Thursday 3 October, 2013) http://www.theguardian.com/politics/reality-check/2013/oct/03/gay–britain–what–do–statistics–say.

[21] Rose Eveleth, *What Percentage of the Population is Gay? More Than You Think* (Smithsonian.com, October 2013)

http://www.smithsonianmag.com/smart–news/what–percent–of–the–population–is–gay–more–than–you–think–5012467/?no–ist.

22 The Lancet.com
http://www.thelancet.com/action/showFullTableImage?tableId=tbl4&pii
=S0140673613620358.

Chapter 5: What the Bible Has to Say

[1] Romans 1:26–27.
[2] I am counting the story in Judges 19 as one of the seven passages.
[3] Jesus' reference to Sodom and Gomorrah in Matthew 10:15 certainly places what happened in the context of hospitality, though in the letter to Jude (v. 7), the emphasis is clearly on sexual immorality.
[4] Isaiah 1:10; 3:9; Jeremiah 23:14, Ezekiel 16:49.
[5] Walter Brueggemann, *Genesis*, Interpretation: A Bible Series for Teaching and Preaching (Atlanta, John Knox Press, 1982), p. 164.
[6] Richard B. Hays, *The Moral Vision of the New Testament: Community, Cross, New Creation: A Contemporary Introduction to New Testament* (New York, NY, HarperCollins, 1996), p. 381.
[7] James V. Brownson, *Bible Gender Sexuality: Reframing the Church's Debate on Same–Sex Relationships* (Grand Rapids, MI, Eerdmanns Publishing, 2013) p. 268.
[8] Gordon D. Fee & Douglas Stuart, *How to Read the Bible for All its Worth*, 2nd edition (Grand Rapids, MI, Scripture Union, 1994) pp. 151–2.
[9] Hays, p. 381.
[10] Brownson, p. 270.
[11] *IVP New Bible Dictionary*, ed. By J. D. Douglas and others, 2nd edition (Leicester, Inter–Varsity Press, 1982) p. 488.
[12] Brownson, p. 272.
[13] Jerome Murphy O'Connor, *1 Corinthians*, The People's Bible Commentary (Oxford, The Bible Reading Fellowship, 1997) p. 59.
[14] Q. in Hays, 382.
[15] Hays, p. 383.
[16] Originally I suggested pederasty here as the most likely reference of *arsenokoitai*. I have since updated the manuscript (July 2019) to indicate other possibilities.
[17] Brownson, p. 274.
[18] Timothy Keller, *Romans 1–7 For You* (New Malden, UK: The Good Book Company, 2014) p. 32.
[19] Romans 1:26–27.

[20] James Alison, 'But the Bible says...' A Catholic Reading of Romans 1 (2004) http://www.jamesalison.co.uk/texts/eng15.html.
[21] Hays, p. 26–27.
[22] Brownson. pp. 85–109.
[23] Hays, p. 389.

Chapter 6: A Lot of Trust in a Book With a Talking Snake

[1] Terence Copley, *About the Bible: Questions anyone might ask about its origins, nature and purpose* (Guildford, UK: Bible Society, 1990) pp. 1–7.
[2] To get a feel for the political dimension of early church discussions, see Henry Chadwick, *The Early Church: The Penguin History of the Church* (Middlesex, England: Penguin Books, 1967), pp. 133–145, or Peter Frankopan, *The Silk Roads: A New History of the World* (London: Bloomsbury Paperbacks, 2015), pp. 51–54.
[3] Deuteronomy 20 and Joshua 6.
[4] For a good presentation of the latter view, see Nick Spencer and Denis Alexander, Rescuing Darwin: God and Evolution in Britain Today in *Theos, The Public Theology Think Tank* (Theos, 2009).
[5] See Genesis 1–3 for the stories of Creation and The Fall.
[6] See for example Psalm 137.
[7] Isaiah 2:4.

Chapter 7: Framing the Same-Sex Discussion Within the 'Big Story'

[1] Richard B. Hays, *The Moral Vision of the New Testament: A Contemporary Introduction to New Testament Ethics*, (New York: Harper Collins, 1996), p. 389.
[2] Karl Barth, *Church Dogmatics, Vol III, pt 4*, (T&T Clark, Edinburgh), p. 184.
[3] Steve Chalke, A Matter of Integrity: The Church, Sexuality, Inclusion and an Open Conversation, Amazon Kindle e-book, (location 67 of 565).
[4] James V. Brownson, *Bible Gender Sexuality: Reframing the Church's Debate on Same–Sex Relationships* (Grand Rapids, MI, Eerdmanns Publishing, 2013), pp. 86–90.
[5] Dale C. Allison, *The Sermon on the Mount: Inspiring the Moral Imagination* (New York, NY: The Crossroads Publishing Company, 1999), p. 79.
[6] Matthew 19:8
[7] Allison, pp. 79–83.

[8] Steve Clifford, *The Bible and Homosexuality: a response to Steve Chalke*, available on the Evangelical Alliance Website: http://www.eauk.org/church/stories/the–bible–and–homosexuality.cfm.
[9] Hays, pp. 193–200.
[10] Hays, pp. 391–394
[11] Hays, pp. 391–392
[12] Hays, pp. 392–393.
[13] Hays, pp. 393–394.
[14] Wesley Hill, *Washed and Waiting: Reflections on Christian Faithfulness and Homosexuality* (Grand Rapids: Zondervan, 2010), pp. 131–150.

Chapter 8: Group Conversation—Session Two

[1] Premier Radio, *Rob Bell debates Andrew Wilson,* part of the series Unbelievable, (interview led by Senior ed. Justin Brierley): http://www.premier.org.uk/radio/Shows/Saturday/Unbelievable/Videos/Rob-Bell-debates-Andrew-Wilson.
[2] Premier Radio, 16:15—20:46 minutes into the interview.
[3] Alpha is a well–known, national recognised course for those who are interested in finding out about the Christian faith.

Chapter 11: Group Conversation—Session Three

[1] Jennell Williams Paris, *The End of Sexual Identity: Why Sex is Too Important to Define Who We Are* (Downers Grove, IL: IVP, 2011) pp. 74–76.
[2] Paris, pp. 42.
[3] Ed Shaw, *The Plausibility Problem: The Church and Same–Sex Attraction* (Nottingham, IVP, 2015), pp. 35–43.
[4] See http://eve–tushnet.blogspot.com/2010_06_01_archive.html#1921445070183139.
[5] Shaw, p. 36.
[6] Paris, p. 51.

Chapter 12: The First Gay Marriages & Some Honest Engagement

[1] https://www.youtube.com/watch?v=q9pOJ8Bc_–g.

Chapter 14: Group Conversation—Session Four

[1] Allison, pp. 5–6.

[2] William J. Webb, *Slaves, Women & Homosexuals: Exploring the Hermeneutics of Cultural Analysis* (Illinois: InterVarsity Press, 2001), pp. 30–66.

[3] Webb, pp. 53–55.

[4] Webb, p. 84.

[5] Steve Chalke, *A Matter of Integrity: The Church, Sexuality, Inclusion and an Open Conversation,* Amazon Kindle e–book, (ref. 20, location 446).

[6] Steve Holmes, *Homosexuality and Hermeneutics: Creating Counter Cultural Communities* (eauk, 2013): http://www.eauk.org/church/stories/homosexuality–and–hermeneutics.cfm.

[7] Webb, pp. 87–90.

[8] www.spiritualfriendship.org.

[9] Oliver O'Donovan, *Church in Crisis: The Gay Controversy and the Anglican Communion* (Eugene, OR: Wipf and Stock Publishers, 2008), p. 108.

[10] Scot McKnight, *The Blue Parakeet: Rethinking How You Read the Bible* (Grand Rapids, MI: Zondervan, 2008), pp. 29–35.

[11] McKnight, pp. 159–162.

Chapter 15: Group Conversation—Session Five

[1] A further statement has been made by the Baptist Union Council (March 16) urging (humbly) all our churches, for the sake our unity to refrain from conducting same–sex marriages 'out of mutual respect'. This is clearly a step further than before in the advice being given to our churches by the Council—for recent discussion see http://www.baptist.org.uk/Articles/463873/Baptist_Union_Council.aspx.

[2] Beth Ann Gaede (ed) *Congregations Talking about Homosexuality* (Durham, MC: Alban Institute Publishing,1998), p. viii.

[3] O'Donovan, pp. 118–119.

[4] O'Donovan, pp. 115–119.

Printed in Poland
by Amazon Fulfillment
Poland Sp. z o.o., Wrocław

52861127R00113